THE
DUDE ABIDES

THE GOSPEL ACCORDING
TO THE COEN BROTHERS

CATHLEEN FALSANI

ZONDERVAN.com/
AUTHOR**TRACKER**
follow your favorite authors

ZONDERVAN

The Dude Abides
Copyright © 2009 by Cathleen Falsani

This title is also available as a Zondervan ebook. Visit www.zondervan.com/ebooks.

This title is also available in a Zondervan audio edition. Visit www.zondervan.fm.

Requests for information should be addressed to:

Zondervan, *Grand Rapids, Michigan* 49530

Library of Congress Cataloging-in-Publication Data

Falsani, Cathleen, 1970–
    The dude abides : the Gospel according to the Coen brothers / Cathleen Falsani.
      p. cm.
    Includes bibliographical references.
    Includes filmography.
    ISBN 978-0-310-29246-3 (softcover)
    1. Coen, Ethan—Criticism and interpretation. 2. Coen, Joel—Criticism and
interpretation. I. Title.
    PN1998.3C6635F35   2009
    791.4302'330922—dc22   2009018440

Published in association with Yates & Yates, www.yates2.com.

Interior design by Beth Shagene
Cover and interior illustrations by Erik Rose

Printed in the United States of America

10 11 12 13 14 15 • 23 22 21 20 19 18 17 16 15 14 13 12 11 10 9 8 7 6 5 4

For my father, Mario,
who took me to see my first movie,
The Apple Dumpling Gang, *in 1975,*
when I was not quite five years old,
and instilled in me a lifelong love of film.
Thank you, Daddy.

CONTENTS

FOREWORD

BY RABBI ALLEN SECHER

I'd like to suggest a movie scenario to the Coen brothers. It is the story of a young arrogant boy who insists he can single-handedly defeat his country's greatest terrorist. He's called on his boast. He approaches the enemy's weapon of mass destruction with a laser beam of his own invention, and with a few blasts it is vaporized. Frightened at the prospect of imminent defeat, the enemy retreats back behind its own boundaries.

The kid is a national hero. He's welcomed to the home of the president. Soon after, his friendship with the president's son blossoms into an intimate (some say homosexual) relationship. Countless of the country's rock stars compose tributes to the young hero, and cable channels praise the boy on 24-7 news cycles. He marries the president's daughter. His popularity ratings far exceed the president's own, and soon the president's jealousy builds to homicidal so that the boy must flee. The president takes out a contract on the boy's life. The plot is foiled, and in the gun battle, the president's son is slain. And the president has a heart attack and dies.

The popularity of the boy is so great that he replaces the president. The boy has a guitar talent and appears constantly on nighttime TV playing his own compositions. One day, while sunning himself on the roof of the presidential palace, he gazes down at the mansion's pool and spots an intern lounging poolside. The boy's chief of staff informs him that the beauty is married to one of his generals. The boy immediately dispatches the general to the front lines, where he is quickly killed. Because his country permits multiple marriages, the intern and the boy are soon wed. Their first child dies. When the boy laments, "Why? Why?" his attorney general points out his lust and his role in the death of the general. Fast-forward. Eventually the boy will be challenged for his office unsuccessfully by one of his own sons, and upon his death, another of his sons succeeds him.

Sound like a good plot, right?

Nah, nobody would believe it.

But our biblical ancestors did. It's the story of King David, the man said to have been the apple of God's eye. While most of us cannot imagine a world without cell phones, emails, iPods, and DVDs, our biblical ancestors had none of the above. Their mass communication was through spoken stories and pageantry. The early tales were broadcast via fireside chats while tending sheep, conversations while on pilgrimage, or parents at the bedtime hour. By the time of Moses in the Old Testament, we are introduced to thunder and lightning, the sound of the shofar, and Ten Commandments on a stone slab. Subsequently, we added the role of the *Kohen* (also called the Cohen, Cohn, and Coen) to dramatize the points being made. The high priest surrounded himself with stage props such as fancy clothing, frankincense, burnt offerings, elaborate music, and fiery sacrifices — all to make a moral point.

The historian Josephus informs us that in the post-Maccabean period the high priest was seen as exercising authority in all things — political, legal, and sacerdotal. He was the supreme power. The high priest of the Sanhedrin was also chief judge and president. The *Kohen* became producer extraordinaire. As time went by, the community added the role of the *Darshan*—the storyteller—interpreter of the legends. His job was to make the moral high road come alive to even the mostly ignorant listeners. A musical score was also added to the weekly scriptural reading to enhance its exposition.

Joel and Ethan Coen have become part of the same progression from priest to judge to storyteller to producer extraordinaire. Cathleen calls them secular theologians.

A careful reading of Scripture finds our fathers and mothers dealing with family, love, and marriage; revenge, faith, and fear; rehabilitation, consequences, and commitment; fantasy, sexuality, and violence; dreams, visions, and betrayal; lust, gluttony, and ego; kindness, the unknowable, and respect; compassion, pride, and adultery; murder, idolatry, and double-cross; choices, threats, and doubt. And this list is only a partial one. It's all there in our Sacred Works. Or as Casey Stengel (a.k.a. "The Old Perfessor") would say, "You could look it up."

My guess is that the Coens would deny any message to their medium or that they were theologians at all (secular or otherwise.) Still, the long list of biblical plot points in the above paragraph resonates through each of their films.

Danny Siegel in his book *And God Braided Eve's Hair* sets up one significant Coenesque spiritual message: "If you always assume the person sitting next to you is the Messiah waiting for some simple human kindness, you will soon come to weigh your words and watch your hands. And if he chooses not to be revealed in your time, it will not matter." A messiah yet to be revealed in the world of the Coen brothers could be Barton Fink or Jeffrey "The Dude" Lebowski;

Marge Gunderson, Sheriff Bell, or Chad Feldheimer. The chosen one could be located in the Ukraine, Washington, D.C., Arizona, or Los Angeles. But most likely, he or she is sitting right next to the Coens (and you) at this very moment.

In *The Dude Abides*, Cathleen refers to the commentator Rashi (an acronym for Rabbi Solomon bar Isaac), who commented on every biblical and Talmudic nuance. Cathleen has become the Rashi to the Coens' scripture. The brothers' cinematic oeuvre is filled with lessons learned, morals attended, and complex characters straight out of the biblical playbook. If it was only by osmosis that they incorporated their theology while daydreaming in Hebrew school in Minneapolis, we still are grateful for their training. If Joel and Ethan ever decide on pursuing second careers in theology, there are a few rabbinic schools I would like to recommend.

Rabbi Allen Secher is presently serving as rabbi for Bet Harim Jewish Community of the Flathead Valley, Montana. Ordained in 1961, Rabbi Secher has served congregations in Chicago, Los Angeles, Mexico City, New York, and Bozeman, Montana. In addition to his rabbinic work, he has been an actor, television producer, documentary filmmaker, and radio commentator.

THE COEN BROTHERS

A SHORT BIOGRAPHY

JOEL COEN

The older of the two Coen boys, Joel Coen was born on November 29, 1954, in St. Louis Park, Minnesota (a suburb of Minneapolis), to Edward and Rena Coen. Edward was a professor of economics at the University of Minnesota and Rena a professor of fine arts at St. Cloud State University. The family is Jewish, and Joel and his siblings (the brothers have an older sister, Debbie, who became a doctor and moved to Israel) grew up attending synagogue and Hebrew school. After spending his last year of high school at Simon's Rock in Great Barrington, Massachusetts, a uniquely progressive school that allowed its students to take college classes during what would have been their high school years, Joel attended New York University's undergraduate film program. After graduating from NYU, Joel worked as a production assistant for industrial films and music videos, before landing his first feature film gig as an assistant editor on his friend Sam Raimi's 1981 horror flick, *The Evil Dead*. In 1984, Joel wrote and directed his first feature film, *Blood Simple*, with his brother, Ethan. The film starred the young actress Frances McDormand, who married Joel after the film's release in 1984 and went on to appear in six more Coen brothers' films. With Ethan, Joel has been nominated for nine Academy Awards (including two under the name Roderick Jaynes, the alias the duo uses for its film editing credits). The Coens have won two screenwriting Oscars, for

Fargo and *No Country for Old Men*, and received their first Oscars for Best Achievement in Directing and Best Picture in 2008 for *No Country for Old Men*.

ETHAN COEN

Three years his brother's junior, Ethan Coen was born on September 21, 1957, in St. Louis Park, Minnesota. After following in his brother's footsteps at Simon's Rock, Ethan, always the more conscientious student, enrolled at Princeton University, where he studied philosophy. In his senior university thesis, "Two Views of Wittgenstein's Later Philosophy," he wrote that he thought it "the height of stupidity" to believe in God. Despite his claims of disbelief, spiritual themes recur often in Ethan's extra-cinematic writings, including his 1998 short story collection, *Gates of Eden*, and an off-Broadway production of three one-act plays, 2008's *Almost an Evening* (in which Oscar winner F. Murray Abraham was cast as an angry God). Since the brothers' feature-film debut in 1984, Ethan has been listed as producer to Joel's director in their film credits, though the brothers say they share equally in both endeavors. Ethan has been married to film editor Tricia Cooke since 1992.

THE COEN BROTHERS

FILMOGRAPHY

Blood Simple (1984)

Raising Arizona (1987)

Miller's Crossing (1990)

Barton Fink (1991)

The Hudsucker Proxy (1993)

Fargo (1996)

The Big Lebowski (1997)

O Brother, Where Art Thou? (2000)

The Man Who Wasn't There (2001)

Intolerable Cruelty (2003)

The Ladykillers (2004)

No Country for Old Men (2007)

Burn After Reading (2008)

A Serious Man (2009)

Have patience with everything unresolved in your heart and try to love the questions themselves, as if they were locked rooms or books written in a very foreign language. Don't search for answers, which could not be given to you now, because you would not be able to live them. And the point is to live everything. Live the question now. Perhaps then, some day far in the future, you will gradually without even noticing it, live your way to the answer.

Rainer Maria Rilke, *Letters to a Young Poet*

ELUCIDATING THE *LUCIDA*

AN INTRODUCTION

God is swearing at me.

Seated in the second row at the Bleecker Street Theatre in New York City, I am, in fact, close enough to this raging Jehovah that I'm tempted to dodge the sacred spittle he's spraying along with a litany of not-so-holy expletives. This is the Angry God of Old Testament fame, the smiter-in-chief and jealous deity, the one with the long white beard, Birkenstocks, and flowing robes who's had it up to here with humans complaining, disobeying his commandments, and generally being a collective pain in the tuckus.

Watching this Angry God — portrayed oh-so-divinely by Oscar winner F. Murray Abraham — rant and rave about his creation in the third act of Ethan Coen's off-Broadway production of three religiously themed mini-plays called *Almost an Evening*, I begin to reconsider the wisdom of mining the treasure trove that is the Coen brothers' cinematic oeuvre for spiritual gems. If the overarching spiritual message of Joel and Ethan Coen's twenty-five-year contribution to film is that God doesn't exist and we're all screwed — or, worse still, that God exists all right and boy is he pissed — then the book you're reading would be both short and, to borrow a favorite expression from one of the Coens' most enduring characters, "a bummer, man."

My fears are allayed when a second deity — played with abundant grace and good humor by Mark Linn-Baker — takes the stage in a natty suit and bow tie, smiling kindly. This God is of a more recent, New Testament vintage, and he reassures the audience that we are loved and all we must do to find peace and direction is reach out to God. Everything's gonna be all right, he soothes. As you might imagine, Angry God does not take kindly to this rival Almighty and threatens to kick his butt. The exchange that follows is hilarious, poking fun not at God but at our sometimes schizophrenic perceptions of God. What Ethan Coen seems to be saying is that often what we believe about God is more a projection of our own needs or desires than what and who God might actually be. Be aware of the lens through which you view the Almighty, the playwright chides: before you invoke a divine imprimatur, make sure it's divine and not comically (or tragically) human.

Since their directorial debut in 1984 with the neo-thriller *Blood Simple*, the Minnesota-bred writing-directing-producing team of Joel and Ethan Coen has created some of the most quirky, enigmatic, and enduring films of my generation. Beginning with *Blood Simple*, the story of a man who has grave doubts about his wife's fidelity and what happens when he attempts to uncover the "truth," the Coens have boldly engaged serious existential questions with darkly intelligent humor. Many of their films are riotously funny and eminently quotable—just ask anyone who is a fan of *Raising Arizona* or *The Big Lebowski*—while others are somber noir treatments of other classical genres from romantic comedy to gangland drama. Each of their fourteen feature-length films is marked by theological, philosophical, and mythological touchstones that enrich even the slapstickiest moments. Each film probes confounding ethical and spiritual quandaries, giving us a tour of nuanced moral universes that may be individual (in the case of *Barton Fink*), geographic (as in *Fargo*), or historic (such as the Depression era of *O Brother, Where Art Thou?*).

It would be dishonest to try to wrestle the Coen brothers' films into a God-shaped box—or wood chipper, for that matter—and that is not my intention. I do, however, take seriously their invitation to wrestle with important spiritual and moral questions. It is in that dialogical spirit that I want to uncover what the overarching spiritual messages of their films—their "gospel," if you will—might be. While it is clear that the Coens are artists, not preachers, I agree wholeheartedly with one astute critic who calls them "secular theologians" whose body of work is "one of the most sneakily moralistic in recent American cinema."[1] While the spiritual content of their films is fairly evident, I don't want to infer from that an intention by the filmmakers to teach us some sort of spiritual lesson. Their films are like life itself, full of questions with little didacticism. Still, the Coens leave the door to interpretation (spiritual, artistic, stylistic, and otherwise) wide open. To paraphrase something Ethan told Charlie Rose in an interview after *No Country for Old Men* was released, the Coens' films are "something more than that, but that."

There is a moral order to the worlds the Coens create. Whether the story is a farcical crime caper or an American gothic tale of betrayal, there always are consequences to the characters' actions, for better or for worse. Bad guys are punished and the decent are rewarded for their innate goodness, though beware the viewer who assumes it will be easy to discern which is which. Sins come to light; lies and deception are revealed for what they are. It may even happen occasionally that the hand of God intervenes to restore order from chaos.

The Coens' films are visually stunning, with certain leitmotifs, or recurring themes, that repeat in nearly every story. Often, the opening frames of the films depict long, empty roads or sweeping shots of tall trees or skyscrapers, symbolizing, perhaps, the horizontal relationship between one human being and another, and the vertical relationship between humans and the Divine. The filmmakers often play with light and dark, drawing on Roland Barthes's notion of *camera lucida*—that the viewer is deeply and personally affected by the images he or she sees. Our interpretation is just that—ours. It is personal; we project our own ideas onto the story, just as the film's images are projected onto the screen.

The Coens are virtuoso wordsmiths in love with language and wordplay. The dialogue in their films is rich, nuanced, and playful, awash with allusions, cultural homage, and inside jokes. It is intriguing to speculate how much Ethan's undergraduate studies in philosophy at Princeton University might have influenced his approach to the spoken word. In 1979, Ethan wrote his senior thesis on the later works of the Austrian philosopher Ludwig Wittgenstein, whose major emphasis was on the philosophy of language. Wittgenstein argued that what we can think is contingent on what we can say, that thought flows from language, and not the other way around. If not, we're just making noise.

In his Princeton thesis, Ethan discusses the idea of meaning by explaining the difference between understanding and sympathizing. "If it's a question of my understanding/not understanding their beliefs, rather than my feeling sympathy/not feeling sympathy with their attitude as manifested in their avowals of belief, then yes, I *understand* what it means to say that there is an omnipotent, benevolent creator, and that claim strikes me as the height of stupidity," he wrote.[2] Perhaps this understanding of language and meaning has allowed the Coens to write eloquently about spiritual or metaphysical beliefs they don't necessarily hold.

One persistent criticism of the Coens' work is that it is all style without any soul. To my mind, this seems like missing the forest for the trees. With the charge of style, I agree wholeheartedly. What such critics fail to appreciate is the transcendent meaning rife in all their films. Even those that appear merely silly or frivolous on the surface contain elegant — and often self-deprecatingly humorous — glimpses of true grace amid worlds dominated by greed, malice, and inhumanity. The Coens often juxtapose comical scenes with brutal depictions of violence that stun us into considering the consequences of what we believe and how we act. It's as if by exploring with an unblinking eye the worst of humanity — the darkest of evil — the light, the goodness, shines even brighter. Their films often echo songwriter Bruce Cockburn's insistence that we must "kick at the darkness until it bleeds daylight."

Some people of faith likely will take issue with the entire premise of my endeavor here. Why look to secular theologians for perspectives on God, faith, and the life of the Spirit? Christians in particular may object to my application of the word *gospel* to the Coens' overarching worldview. I would urge my coreligionists to keep an open mind. Film is a powerful cultural artifact and translator that transcends — and helps us transcend — racial, economic, and religious divides. "Film is the language of this new generation," my friend Lee Strobel, author of *The Case for Christ*, told me recently. "It's the way in which they communicate."

Rather than simply condemn films that present points of view with which we disagree or even find abhorrent, we should examine them and seek to grasp the messages they send, messages with which so many viewers find emotional resonance. We should, perhaps, ask why. Maybe we'll learn something.

While the Coens' films seldom reflect a classical Christ-centered worldview, they are an articulate reflection of the spiritual and existential sensibilities of many of our brothers and sisters of different faith traditions and of none. Do not be afraid of the darkness; without it, light wouldn't exist. To quote another of my generation's great secular theologians, U2, in their song "God Part II": "Don't believe the devil; I don't believe his book. But the truth is not the same without the lies he made up." A kernel of truth will rise above a mountain of lies, just as even a single spark pierces the darkness. And all truth is God's truth, no matter where it comes from or who's saying it.

The beauty of art is, of course, that it's open to interpretation and moreover that it *requires* interpretation. What I see may not be what you see, and that is as it should be. Art demands interpretation, and each work of art exists in a field of possible interpretations, but that field is not infinite. As you travel with me on this tour of the Coen brothers' moral universes, I hope you'll disagree with conclusions that don't ring true to you and draw your own. As the great slacker saint of Los Angeles, Jeffrey "The Dude" Lebowski, so eloquently put it, in the end, "That's just, like, your opinion, man."

Opinions are important, and they are subjective, colored, and shaped by life experiences, predispositions, and points of view. We should be able to disagree, especially when what we're disagreeing about is something that truly matters.

BLOOD SIMPLE

CHAPTER 1

BLOOD SIMPLE

"Down here, you're on your own."

THE FOREST

In an unnamed Texas town, Abby is cheating on her bar-owning husband, Marty. Abby's lover is Ray, one of Marty's bartenders. Marty hires Visser, a sleazy detective, to kill Abby and Ray, but Visser has his own nefarious plans. The plot of this neo-noir crime thriller uncoils in double- and triple-crosses where almost nothing is what it seems, ending in a chillingly violent showdown between Abby, Visser, and the ghosts spawned by her guilty conscience.

THE TREES

Bleak images of rural Texas slowly flip past as day turns to night. A scrap of a blown-out tire lies on a span of an asphalt highway punctuated by yellow demarcation lines. Desiccated brown fields foreground the tall buildings of a nondescript city on the horizon. The black silhouettes of huge oil derricks pierce the hard Texas earth like birds hunting grubs. Finally, the twin headlights of a lone vehicle break the gloom of a dark, rainy stretch of road.

A narrator's voice, dripping with smarmy faux-southern charm, sets the tone:

Narrator: "The world is full of complainers. But the fact is, nothing comes with a guarantee. I don't care if you're the Pope of Rome, President of the United States, or even Man of the Year, something can always go wrong. And go ahead, complain to your neighbor, ask for help—and watch him fly. Now in Russia, they got it mapped out so that everyone pulls for everyone else—that's the theory anyway. But what I know about is Texas, and down here, you're on your own."

Two people, barely visible in silhouette from the vantage point of the backseat, ride in a car in silence through the rain-soaked night. The driver of the car, Ray (John Getz), is chauffeuring Abby (Frances McDormand), the gamine wife of Julian "Marty" Marty (Dan Hedeya), the owner of the roadhouse where he tends bar. Abby is heading for Houston, on the run from her husband. Ray is her getaway man in more ways than one. "He gave me a little pearl-handled .38 for our first anniversary," Abby tells the laconic bartender. "Figure I better leave before I used it on him."

When Ray expresses a modicum of interest in her—"I always liked you," he says—she yells at him to stop the car. Ray figures this is because she recognizes the car that's following them. Instead it's because she's spotted the sign for a motel. "What do you wanna do?" Ray asks. "What do *you* want to do?" she answers. So they make love fitfully in the hollow dankness of a cheap motel room, and the next morning, the phone rings. Abby is still asleep, wrapped in a sheet, so Ray answers. It's Marty. He knows.

Marty is a swarthy, skeevy, ne'er-do-well businessman straight out of central casting. He's been having Abby tailed by a private investigator, figuring she was having an affair but not sure with whom. The private eye is a comical-looking creature, a fat man with a dingy cowboy hat and a leisure suit the shade of lemon-yellow custard, who drives a beat-up Volkswagen Beetle — the same car that had been following Ray's vehicle the night before on the rainy highway. This is Loren Visser (M. Emmet Walsh), though we never hear anyone call him by name. He chews gum while he smokes, grins like a madman, and cracks inappropriate jokes.

The day after Abby's affair is discovered, in Marty's office at the roadhouse, Visser shoves a manila envelope across the desk at Marty, who curtly flips through the black-and-white photographs of his wife in bed with Ray. "I know a place you can get that framed," Visser drawls, snickering.

"What did you take these for?" Marty demands. "You called me, I knew they were there, so what do I need these for?"

"Call it a fringe benefit," Visser cackles, adding that he watched the couple make love most of the night. Marty pays Visser his fee, tossing an envelope stuffed with money at him so that it lands on the floor next to his chair.

Marty: "You know, in Greece they cut off the head of a messenger who brought bad news."

Visser: "Now, that don't make much sense."

Marty: "No. It just made them feel better."

Visser: "Well, first off, Julian, I don't know what the story is in Greece, but in this state we got very definite laws about that. Second place, I ain't a messenger. I'm a private investigator. And third place — and most important — it ain't such bad news. I mean, you thought he was a colored. You're always assuming the worst. Anything else?"

Marty: "Yeah, don't come by here anymore. If I need you again, I know which rock to turn over."

This last biting comment gives Visser pause for a moment, but then he just laughs maniacally, saying, "That's good. 'Which rock to turn over.' That's very good." As Visser ambles to the door, still chuckling at the cuckolded husband, he adds, "Well, gimme a call whenever you wanna cut off my head. I can crawl around without it."

Marty chooses to be cruel to Visser, a man who is far from heroic, but whose presence in Marty's world was a result of Marty's invitation. Visser was merely doing the job Marty hired him to do. The audience is left to wonder, as the tragic events of the rest of the film unfold, whether things would have been different had Marty just paid Visser and left it at that, without verbally attacking Visser as a way of demonstrating his sense of moral superiority.

It's a small, seemingly insignificant choice, one of many that Marty and the other characters make throughout the film that lead to their downfalls. What if Abby had let Ray drive her to Houston as planned without inviting him to spend the night with her at the motel? What if, when he learned that Marty knew about the affair, Ray had walked away from Abby rather than pursue the relationship? What if? We are, the filmmakers seem to be saying, the authors of our own destruction, setting tragedy in motion—or avoiding it altogether—by the smallest decisions to turn, as it were, left instead of right, or to choose to follow our own lustful desires rather than doing the moral, sensible thing.

In the next scene, Ray takes Abby, who decides not to go to Houston after all, to her and Marty's house to collect a few things—namely, that little pearl-handled revolver. Then it's back to his apartment, where Abby waits while Ray runs an errand. Despite her warning him not to do anything stupid, Ray goes to the road-house to confront Marty, who is sitting out back, watching his employees dump empty liquor boxes into a tall incinerator. Ray wants the two-weeks' pay Marty owes him, but Marty refuses to pay, saying, "She's an expensive piece of ass."

The logical step would have been for the two rivals for Abby's affection to come to blows, but Marty engages in mental warfare instead, planting seeds of doubt about Abby's intentions toward Ray. Marty says she's probably sleeping with other people and mocks Ray for believing that Abby stayed in town to be with him. "What's really going to be funny is when she gives you that innocent look and says, 'What're you talkin' about, Ray. I haven't done anything funny.'"

The next morning, Abby wakes up and walks into Ray's living room, where she's surprised to find her dog, Opal, panting and staring at her. Marty appears out of hiding and grabs Abby from behind, lifting her off her feet and dragging her outside with the intention of raping her. Abby, diminutive but feisty, grabs Marty's finger, bending it backward until it breaks with a satisfying crack. She then kicks him in the groin, sending him crawling pathetically across the lawn to retch on his knees.

Marty later tracks down Visser and offers him $10,000 to murder Abby and Ray. Visser, laughing most of the time, agrees and tells Marty to get out of town for a few days. Go to Corpus Christi and go fishing, he suggests. Get noticed.

That night, Visser appears ominously at Ray's apartment window while the illicit couple sleeps. He sneaks inside and steals Abby's .38, then goes back outside. Visser steps up to the window, and we see a flash of light, which we assume is the gun going off. Later, Visser meets with Marty back in his office at the roadhouse, where a string of dead fish sits morbidly on his desk. Again, he shoves across the desk a manila envelope with photographic evidence inside—black-and-white glossies of Ray and Abby in bed with what appear to be gunshot wounds riddling their upper bodies.

Marty is sick to his stomach, rushing to the nearby washroom to retch. (The Coens have an odd preoccupation with vomit, a peculiar leitmotif in many of their films.) Wiping his mouth with the back of his hand, Marty leans into his safe to get Visser's $10,000. What we don't know until later is that Marty has swapped the photo for a sign from the bathroom warning employees to wash their hands. It's the first of many double-crosses that will follow in quick succession as the plot of the film unfolds.

After handing over the cash, Visser asks Marty if he's been "very, very careful" about covering up his tracks. When Marty says he has, Visser shoots him in the chest with Abby's pearl-handled .38, drops the gun on the floor next to Marty's body, and leaves—forgetting to retrieve the Zippo lighter engraved with his name and "Elks Man of the Year" from under the pile of dead fish.

In the next scene, we learn that Abby and Ray are alive and well; Visser has doctored the photographs. The flash we saw that night outside Ray's apartment was a flashbulb from the private detective's camera. Ray leaves Abby at an apartment she's rented in town and returns to the roadhouse to try to collect the money Marty owes him. He discovers Marty's body and, seeing Abby's .38 on the floor, assumes she's killed him.

Instead of calling the police, Ray tries to clean up the bloody mess before hauling Marty's body to his car and driving off to bury him. Having second thoughts, Ray pulls over by a field on a long, empty stretch of road and runs away in a panic. When he returns to the car a few moments later, Marty's body is no longer in the backseat. Marty, it transpires, is not quite dead and has managed to crawl away from the car.

Ray drags Marty to the field, digs a hole, throws him in, and buries him alive. Thinking he was covering up his lover's murder, Ray becomes a murderer himself. He turns up at Abby's apartment some time later, clearly shaken, and tells her that he's "cleaned it all up." She has no idea what he's talking about. Frightened and confused, she says, "What're you talkin' about, Ray? I haven't done anything funny."

At last, Marty's words of warning come back to haunt Ray, and he starts to think Abby is playing him for the fool. The phone rings and Abby answers, but the caller says nothing. She assumes it's Marty and tells Ray as much. Ray, of course, assumes she's lying to him and storms out, telling her she "left her weapon behind" at the bar.

That night, alone in her cavernous apartment, Abby dreams that Marty appears—alive and menacing. "I love you," he says. "I love you too," she answers. "You're just saying that because you're scared," he growls, and adds, "You left your weapon behind," tossing the revolver at her. When she lunges to catch it, she sees that it's her makeup compact. Marty then doubles over in front of her, vomiting blood—and she awakens, covered in sweat.

In the morning, Abby goes to find Ray at his apartment. His belongings are in boxes, and he informs her that he's leaving town. When she asks why, he says he figured it's what she wanted. He asks her to come with him, but she says she first needs to know the truth. Abby assumes that Ray went to the bar to get his money from Marty, the two had a fight, and Ray killed Marty in self-defense. Ray tells

Abby that Marty was killed with her gun. They're both confused and, stammering, Ray confesses: "The truth is, he was alive when I buried him." Abby runs away.

In the next scene, Ray returns yet again to the roadhouse, where someone has tried to break into the safe. Ray finds hidden inside the safe the doctored photograph of him and Abby in bed with gunshot wounds. He's starting to put things together, and when he gets in his car to drive away, he spots a man — Visser — watching him from his VW parked down the block.

Ray goes to Abby's apartment and waits there in the dark, staring out the enormous picture window. Abby walks in and turns the light on, but Ray shouts at her to turn it off because someone's watching. She does but then turns it back on, demanding an explanation of what's happened to Marty, and then Ray is blown forward by a rifle blast to the back, killing him.

Visser is perched atop the building across the street, shooting into the illuminated apartment. Abby cowers in the corner, throwing her shoe at the one exposed lightbulb until it breaks. Visser enters the apartment while Abby, thinking it's Marty come to kill her, flees to the bathroom. Visser rifles through Ray's pockets looking for his photograph — and, presumably, the missing Zippo that he left in Marty's office and thinks Ray has discovered and pocketed. Finding nothing, he stalks the apartment looking for Abby. When he enters the bathroom, it's empty.

Abby has managed to crawl out of the small bathroom window, onto a narrow ledge, and into the room next door. Visser reaches through the window, groping blindly, and Abby drives a knife into his hand, impaling it on the window ledge. Visser's agonized screams are horrific. He begins to shoot through the wall, illuminating Abby's dark hiding place with narrow shafts of light. He finally manages to shoot a big enough hole in the wall to reach through and pull the knife out of his hand. Abby runs into the corridor between the rooms, grabs her gun and trains it at the bathroom door. When she senses movement, she shoots, and we hear Visser's body drop to the floor.

"I ain't afraid of you, Marty," she says.

Mortally wounded and staring up at the sweating bathroom pipes, Visser cackles a wicked, crazy laugh and shouts, "If I see him, I'll sure give him the message." The film ends as the Four Tops begin to sing, "It's the same old song, but with a different meaning since you been gone."

Blood Simple takes its title from a line in Dashiell Hammett's masterful hard-boiled detective novel *Red Harvest*, in which the term *blood simple* is used to describe a kind of mania that takes over when people are exposed to bloody violence. The Coens' debut film is in many ways an homage to Hammett and film noir but with decidedly modern twists. *Blood Simple* uses the film noir themes of alienation, uncertainty, subterfuge, and double-cross—but it cleverly subverts and inverts them. Abby is seemingly guileless, hardly the femme fatale of classic noir films, though the men in her life still meet tragedy as a result of her actions. The Coens make effective use of film noir's fascination with light and dark—much of the deception and double-crossing happens under the cover of darkness. Yet, as the Bible says, all that is hidden shall be revealed in the light of day and by the light of truth.[3]

THE MORAL OF THE STORY . . .

Blood Simple is a meditation on free will. No one in the film is co-erced into making mistakes. Their undoing is entirely their own. No one else is to blame. Each character, when presented with a choice to do the right thing, makes the wrong choice—with tragic results. Abby could have gone to Houston as planned and never hooked up with Ray. Ray could have turned her down when she suggested going to the motel. Marty could have divorced Abby without try-ing to seek revenge. Ray could have walked away with the girl and left his two-weeks' pay behind rather than confront Marty. Marty could have paid Visser without insulting him. Ray could have gone to the police when he found Marty's body. Abby could have gone to the police when she suspected Ray of murdering her husband. Each time, the players chose to cover up their sins rather than be exposed.

If just one of them had made the right choice, tragedy might have been averted. Every choice the characters made was pivotal. This reminds me of something the writer Frederick Buechner once said: "All moments are key moments." Buechner follows that thought with another: "Life itself is grace." But there is no divine intervention in the Coens' story—no redemption and no grace. *Blood Simple* is a cautionary tale about actions and reactions, reminding us that ev-erything we do has consequences that cannot be avoided, no matter how hard we try to hide from them.

RAISING ARIZONA

H.I. McDUNNOUGH
NO. 14686
NOV 29 83

CHAPTER 2

RAISING ARIZONA

"Now y'all who're without sin can cast the first stone . . ."

THE FOREST

Repeat offender H. I. "Hi" McDunnough and his police officer wife, Edwina, long to have a child to complete their family. When they can't conceive the old-fashioned way and their efforts to adopt are rebuffed, the couple decides to kidnap one of the quintuplets born to furniture tycoon Nathan Arizona and his wife. Despite efforts to keep the provenance of their little bundle of joy a secret, some friends and colleagues uncover Hi and Edwina's scheme, and each of them plots to claim the child for their own selfish ends. Arizona foolishly hires a scuzzy mercenary to find his missing child, leading to a hilarious if risky quest to return the child to his real mother's loving arms, while Hi and Edwina discover the true meaning of family bonds.

THE TREES

Shortly after *Raising Arizona* debuted in 1987, a group of Christians, led by a Seattle-area pastor, protested that this film encouraged the abuse and objectification of children. The Coen brothers' farce about a childless couple—a petty criminal and his police officer wife who kidnap one of the quintuplets of an Arizona furniture mogul—certainly contains scenes of abuse and objectification. However, claiming the film *encourages* these crimes is akin to arguing that *Thank You for Smoking* is intended to hook audiences into pack-a-day habits. As is always the case with satire and farce—from *Canterbury Tales* to *The Colbert Report*—the real story is known to those who have eyes to see and ears to hear.

Set largely in a trailer park on the outskirts of Tempe, Arizona, during the mid-1980s heyday of the Reagan administration, *Raising Arizona* touches on many themes: family and commitment, love and marriage, revenge and rehabilitation, dreams and visions, fear and faith, law and grace. It is populated by living and breathing cartoon characters—essential for a farce—who execute superhuman feats without suffering the normal human consequences, not unlike Road Runner and Wile E. Coyote. The protagonist, Hi McDunnough (Nicolas Cage), is an archetypical holy fool, a simple if not entirely simpleminded man whose sweet nature weathers several stints in prison without becoming tainted by cynicism and bitterness. Like the Road Runner cartoon character tattooed on his arm, Hi endures all manner of physical trials—he's beaten, shot at, dragged behind a motorcycle, and thrown through a wall—and survives relatively unscathed to challenge our preconceived notions of what constitutes justice, mercy, and rebirth.

When the film begins, we meet Hi and Edwina, aka "Ed" (Holly Hunter), in a police station as Hi, in his sartorial constant of disheveled hair and a rumpled Hawaiian shirt, is booked for robbing a mini-mart. He is immediately besotted with Ed, who stiffly barks orders at him. "Turn to the right!" A modern seer, Hi looks past Ed's tough exterior and tells her, "You're a flower, you are. Just a little desert flower."

Through a series of voiceovers, Hi tells us about his life and his struggle to stay on the straight and narrow. "I tried to stand up and fly straight, but it wasn't easy with that sumbitch Reagan in the White House," he says. "I dunno, they say he's a decent man, so maybe his advisers are confused." As far as he is concerned, prison isn't so much a bastion of hardened criminals as it is a kind of sleep-away camp for the down-and-out. "The joint is a lonely place after lockup and lights out, when the last of the cons has been swept away by the sandman," Hi narrates, "but I couldn't help thinkin' that a brighter future lay ahead—a future that was only eight to fourteen months away."

A member of the parole board chastises Hi for being a repeat offender, but he counters that they can't keep him locked up forever because he never uses live ammunition. "I didn't wanna hurt anyone," he explains. Still, Hi battles his criminal nature, tempted time and again to knock over quickie marts rather than hold down a steady job. Before his third tenure in the Maricopa County Maximum Security Correctional Facility for Men, Hi gives Ed (whose fiancé has left her) a tiny engagement ring and vows that he's going to change his life for the better. "OK then, I don't know how you come down on the incarceration question," Hi says, "but I was beginning to think that revenge is the only argument makes any sense." Prison didn't offer Hi any new beginnings or hope for rehabilitation. It was a merely a punishment, pure and simple. His real rehabilitation would occur beyond the prison walls.

Upon his release, Hi, who has courted Ed over the years during his frequent appearances at the police station to be booked for robbing convenience stores, arrives at the police station once again, and the couple soon marries at the VFW hall. Hi gets a job at a local factory (Hudsucker Industries, in fact), and the couple enjoys a kind of wedded bliss that Hi fondly calls "the salad days." Soon, however, the two begin to yearn for more — a family. "Ed felt that havin' a critter was the next logical step. It was all she thought about," Hi explains. "Her point was that there was too much love and beauty for just the two of us. Every day we kept a child out of the world was a day he might later regret havin' missed."

Ardently but without success they try to conceive, until one dark day Ed arrives home, with sirens blaring, and tearfully informs Hi that she is barren. "Her insides were a rocky place where my seed could find no purchase," he says after a visit to the fertility doctor. The couple attempts to adopt, but despite Ed being a twice-decorated officer of the law, Hi's checkered past makes it impossible. "Biology and the prejudices of others conspired to keep us childless," Hi proclaims.

Ed quits her job on the police force, gives up on housekeeping, and sinks into a stultifying depression. Hi's job becomes an exercise in frustration — until the couple sees a news report about quintuplets born to the bombastic furniture mogul Nathan Arizona (Trey Wilson) of Unpainted Arizona and his wife, Florence (Lynne Dumin Kitei).

"We've got more than we can handle," reads the headline of a newspaper story about the Arizona quintuplets. Desperation leads Hi and Ed to concoct a plan to kidnap one of the Arizona babies and raise him as their own. Under the cloak of night, Hi climbs a ladder and crawls through the window of the Arizona family mansion where he is confronted with five nappy-clad toddlers in an enormous crib:

Harry, Barry, Larry, Garry, and Nathan Jr. After a false start—the babies get loose; Hi runs around trying to keep them from making a ruckus and falls down the stairs—he returns to Ed empty-handed. Waiting in the getaway car, Ed shouts, "Go back and get me a toddler! I need a baby, Hi; they got more'n they can handle!" On his second attempt, Hi succeeds in kidnapping Nathan Jr. (T. J. Kuhn), or so they assume. A running joke throughout the film is that no one can tell the quints apart, and even Nathan Arizona Sr. isn't sure which baby has been kidnapped. "I think I got the best one," Hi brags, while Ed has second thoughts. "We are doin' the right thing, aren't we, Hi?" she asks.

In one of his many voice-overs, Hi reveals his rationale for the kidnapping. "Now, y'all who're without sin can cast the first stone. We thought it was unfair some should have so many while others should have so few. With the benefit of hindsight, maybe it wasn't such a hot idea. But at the time, Ed's little plan seemed like the solution to all our problems, and the answer to all our prayers."

Back at the trailer park, Hi proudly shows the smiling baby around the homestead and takes a photo portrait of the new "family unit." "What, are you kiddin'? We got us a family here!" Hi shouts. As the new ersatz parents fall asleep by the side of Nathan Jr.'s crib, the camera cuts to a muddy field in a downpour where two escaped convicts, Gale and Evelle Snopes (played by John Goodman and William Forsythe) emerge, birthlike, from a hole in the middle of the field, covered in muck and screaming. They clean themselves up and turn up on the doorstep of Hi and Ed's trailer. The Snopes brothers were friends of Hi during his prison days, and he's genuinely excited to see the pair. Once Ed learns that they've escaped from prison ("We released ourselves on our own recognizance," Evelle corrects her), she insists that the two leave as soon as possible.

When Hi finally falls asleep, he has a nightmare about a beastlike motorcyclist who looks like an evil Mad Maxx, riding through the desert setting fire to daisies and blowing up bunny rabbits with hand grenades. "I'd drifted off, thinkin' about happiness, birth, and new life, but now I was haunted by a vision of . . ." he says. "He was horrible. A lone biker of the apocalypse, a man with all the powers of hell at his command. He could turn the day into night and lay to waste everything in his path. He was especially hard on the little things, the helpless and the gentle creatures. He left a scorched earth in his wake, befoulin' even the sweet desert breeze that whipped across his brow. I didn't know where he came from or why. I didn't know if he was a dream or a vision. But I feared I myself had unleashed him, for he was the Fury That Would Be as soon as Florence Arizona found her little Nathan gone."

Sure enough, the next morning Mrs. Arizona is inconsolable, and police and FBI agents swarm the Arizona compound, dusting for fingerprints and making a mess of the crime scene. Nathan Arizona Sr. vows revenge on the kidnappers and offers a $25,000 reward for Nathan Jr.'s safe return.

The following day, Hi and Ed entertain company ("decent friends," Ed says before kicking the Snopes brothers out of the trailer for the afternoon). Hi's foreman, Glen (Sam McMurray), his wife, Dot (Frances McDormand), and their five near-feral children come to see the new baby, Nathan Jr. (whom the nervous parents alternate between calling Hi Jr. and Ed Jr.). Glen's idiocy (as a parent and in general), the out-of-control children who rove the trailer and its grounds like a gang of young thugs, and Dot's obsession with having more children to replace the ones who are "too big to cuddle" (as if they were puppies) collectively chip away at whatever modicum of peace of mind Hi had enjoyed after Nathan Jr.'s arrival.

As Dot lists all of the things the baby will need—a pediatrician, immunizations, a savings account, money for orthodontia and Arizona State, and a life insurance policy in case Hi gets run over by a truck—Glen proposes that Hi kick the doldrums by spicing up his love life. "I'm talkin' me and Dot are swingers. I'm talking about wife swappin'!" he grins. Hi punches him in the face, snarling, "Keep your g–dd–ned hands off my wife!" He may be a kidnapper and a thief, but he's no adulterer.

In the evening, while driving with Ed and Nathan Jr., Hi surmises that he has probably lost his job. When they stop at a mini-mart to get some diapers for the baby, Ed stays in the car and reads "Three Little Pigs" to Nathan Jr., while Hi holds up the store clerk (with his unloaded gun). When she realizes what he's up to, Ed jumps into the driver's seat and pulls away, furious—just as Hi is trying to make his escape. A classic caper-movie chase scene follows involving Hi, the teenage clerk (armed with a .357 magnum), the police, a Doberman, and Ed in the family car (with Nathan Jr. strapped into his car seat). Hi manages to get away clean—with the Huggies—but must face the wrath of his wife, who castigates him for returning to his unlawful ways.

That night, Gale and Evelle (who are back at the trailer) suggest Hi could solve the family's financial woes by joining them in robbing the Farmers and Mechanics Bank. Hi reluctantly agrees, and after everyone is asleep, he writes a farewell letter to Ed and Nathan Jr., saying that they'd be better off without him. "I will never be the man that you want me to be, the husband and father that you and

Nathan deserve. Maybe it's my upbringing. Maybe it's just that my genes got screwed up—I don't know. But the events of the last day have showed, amply, that I don't have the strength of character to raise up a family in the manner befitting a responsible adult, and not like the wild man from Borneo. I say all this to my shame.... Better I should go, send you money, and let you curse my name. Your loving Herbert."

Meanwhile, we meet the Lone Biker (Randall 'Tex' Cobb) as he pays a visit to Nathan Arizona Sr., introduces himself as Leonard Smalls, and says that he is a manhunter who can find Nathan Jr. Smalls demands more than the $25,000 reward money Arizona is offering, saying that a healthy baby boy will fetch far more than that on the black market. Arizona tells him to get lost and threatens to call the police.

Back at the trailer, Hi's foreman, Glen, shows up before Hi can leave his farewell letter for Ed and skip town. Glen tells Hi that he's fired him and that he knows the baby is the kidnapped Arizona quint. Glen tries to blackmail Hi, saying he'll go to the authorities unless Hi turns over the baby to him and his wife. "Looks like that baby's gonna be Glen Jr. from now on!" Glen says. "I'll give you a day to break the news to Ed."

Overhearing Hi's confrontation with Glen, the Snopes brothers decide to kidnap Nathan Jr. themselves. Hi puts up a valiant fight, wrecking the trailer in the process, but Gale and Evelle get away with the baby. They stop at a gas station for Huggies, and Evelle holds up the clerk. While fleeing the scene, they leave Nathan Jr. in his car seat in the middle of the road. Distraught at endangering the toddler by leaving him behind, Evelle makes Gale promise that they can keep him forever and call him Gale Jr.

But even as the two proceed to the Farmers and Mechanics Bank, Smalls has picked up their trail. Hi and his distraught wife (wearing her police uniform) also are in hot pursuit of the simpleton Snopes brothers. In the car, Ed tells Hi that even if they manage to get Nathan Jr. back, she doesn't want to go on living with him. "We don't deserve Nathan Jr. any more than those jailbirds do," she says, "and if I'm as selfish and irresponsible as you, if I'm as bad as you, what good are we to each other? You and me's just a fool's paradise."

Evelle and Dale manage to pull off the bank robbery, with Nathan Jr. in tow, but as they drive away, they once again realize they've left the baby behind—this time in the parking lot. As they spin the car around to go collect the baby, a canister filled with blue paint explodes inside the money bag, and they wreck the car—just as Hi and Ed pull up. The couple speeds toward the baby, but Smalls gets there first, snatches the baby, and puts him (in his car seat) on the handlebars of his motorcycle.

Confronting Smalls on the road, Ed, unarmed and unafraid, screams, "Gimme that baby, you warthog from hell!" as she snatches Nathan Jr. from his car seat and runs toward the bank. Smalls follows on his motorcycle, but Hi, wielding a two-by-four, knocks him off the bike so Ed can escape. Hi and Smalls engage in hand-to-hand combat, with the bestial biker getting the better of the lanky ex-con. Just as Smalls is about to dispatch Hi with two cocked sawed-off shotguns, we see that Hi has pulled the pin from one of the hand grenades attached to Small's leather vest. Before the bounty hunter can toss the grenade away, it explodes, blowing him to literal bits. "I'm sorry," Hi mouths.

We never know for sure whether Smalls was real or a figment of Hi's imagination, a projection of his worst self and greatest fears.

Either way, it's clear that Hi needed to vanquish Smalls to pursue his dream of a life with Ed.

Having had more than enough, Ed and Hi decide to return Nathan Jr. to his rightful family. While placing the baby back in his crib at the Arizona mansion, Nathan Sr. enters the room, confronting the couple. Hi says they rescued the baby from Smalls, and Nathan Sr. offers them the reward money. Ed says they don't want the money and asks if she can just look at the baby for a few more minutes. Seeing Hi stand with his arm around Ed at the crib's edge, Nathan Sr. realizes that they were the ones who took the baby. The couple confesses, each taking sole responsibility for the crime. Arizona says he won't call the authorities because there was no real harm done, but he wants to know why they did it. Ed tells him it was because they couldn't have children of their own.

Taking pity on them, Nathan Sr. says, "Well, lookit. If you can't have kids you gotta just keep tryin' and hope medical science catches up with you. Like Florence 'n' me — it caught up with a vengeance. And hell, even if it never does, you still got each other." Hi tells him that, unfortunately, it looks like he and Ed are going to split up. Nathan Sr. urges them not to, telling Ed, "Well, ma'am, I don't know much, but I do know human bein's. You brought back my boy so you must have your good points too." As they prepare to leave, climbing back down the ladder Hi originally used to kidnap Nathan Jr., Nathan Sr. counsels them to not make another stupid mistake by splitting up and to sleep on it at least for one more night.

Back at the wrecked trailer, Hi has another dream, this one about the future. He sees Nathan Jr. grown up, a football hero, and hopes that perhaps he and Ed might have contributed a tiny bit to his success. Hi sees further into his own future, to when a much older version of himself and Ed are visited by children and grandchildren —a vision of domestic bliss. "I don't know, you tell me. This whole dream, was it wishful thinking? Was I just fleein' reality, like I know I'm liable to do?" Hi wonders. "And it seemed real. It seemed like us. And it seemed like, well, our home. If not Arizona, then a land, not too far away, where all parents are strong and wise and capable, and all children are happy and beloved. I dunno, maybe it was Utah." With that, the credits roll.

THE MORAL OF THE STORY ...

Hi McDunnough, the holy fool whose spirit is willing but whose flesh is weak, has lived his whole life as a prisoner. Sometimes as a literal prisoner, sometimes a figurative one—but always a prisoner of his own fears, the expectations of others, and his basest instincts. Perhaps the unexpected grace and kind words from a most unlikely source—Nathan Arizona Sr.—have set him free at last from the prison of his own making.

Amid its humor, *Raising Arizona* has many serious things to say about children. They are for many of us a *tabula rasa* onto which we project our hopes and fears. For those of us who want children but have yet to be blessed with them, the ache of their absence can be all-consuming as well as blinding. We want to feel worthy of parenthood, of being entrusted with ushering new souls through this world of ours, instilling in them values that matter, unconditional love, and even our own tastes, predilections, and points of view.

One of my dearest friends, Jen, finds much spiritual solace in *Raising Arizona*. When she and her husband, David, adopted their youngest daughter from Guatemala a few years ago, Hi's words rang in her mind. "I think we got the best one," she told David when they met Mimi for the first time. What that meant to Jen was that her family had been blessed with the child God meant for them to have. They couldn't have orchestrated it or controlled the person that Mimi has turned out to be. They could only shower her with love and support and let God do the rest. (Personally, I think they *did* get the very best one.)

At the end of *Raising Arizona*, despite stumbling over their own will and need to control what is truly uncontrollable, Hi and Ed discover no real harm is done, with the exception of Smalls, who may or may not be an actual person. (The audience is left to wonder whether Smalls is a real person or simply the imaginary projection of Hi's very real fears and self-doubts.) All is put right. Hi has subdued his dark side, the one that wants to ignore the law (whether it's God's or human law or both) and take matters into its own hands. And maybe Hi and Ed really do live happily ever after, whether in the less-than-perfect Arizona of their making or in the Utah of their dreams.

CHAPTER 3

MILLER'S CROSSING

"Nobody knows anybody. Not that well."

THE FOREST

Gangland warfare rages in the Prohibition-era city ruled by Irish mob boss Leo O'Bannon and his consigliere Tom Reagan. Tom is furious when Leo refuses the request of would-be Italian godfather Johnny Caspar, who wants to place a hit on Jewish bookie Bernie Bernbaum.

Leo is in love with Verna, Bernie's sister. Unbeknownst to Leo, however, Verna and Tom are having a torrid affair. When Tom reveals his involvement with Verna, Leo throws his consigliere out of his outfit, and Tom agrees to make an alliance with Caspar—or at least that's what Tom wants everyone to believe. When Caspar orders Tom to kill Bernie, he balks, and Caspar's henchman, Eddie the Dane, begins to get suspicious of Tom's true allegiances.

Tom takes Bernie out to the woods to execute him, but afterward no one is certain whether Tom has gone through with it, whether Bernie is dead or alive. Verna searches for the truth about her brother's disappearance, Leo searches for the truth about who is really loyal to him, and Tom searches for the truth of his own heart—if he can uncover it beneath all of his emotional armor.

THE TREES

*I stood among them, but not of them;
in a shroud of thoughts which were not their thoughts.*

Lord Byron

The life of the mind is our most private haven. No one can know our thoughts unless we choose to share them. In *Miller's Crossing*, Tom Reagan (Irish actor Gabriel Byrne) conceals his beneath a fedora that serves as his stoic's crown. Tom is smart, the most intelligent of all the nefarious characters in the film, and he is ruled almost exclusively by reason despite living within the confines of a sometimes-brutal criminal enterprise. While he certainly is armed and dangerous, Tom, unlike many of the gangsters in the film, keeps his aggression in check, killing only when necessary. He attacks only to protect himself or someone he loves, not for vendetta or ego. He acts with considered purpose, weighing the consequences of his actions even if he refuses to share his complicated reasoning with anyone else.

The film begins with ice tumbling into the lowball glass of whiskey that is Tom's ever-present security blanket. We see the drink before we see Tom, who moves to his post behind his boss, the Irish gangster Liam "Leo" O'Bannon (Albert Finney), from which he stares wordlessly at the Italian crime boss and Leo's rival Johnny Caspar (Jon Polito).

Caspar has come to see Leo to complain about the Jewish numbers runner Bernie Bernbaum (John Turturro). Caspar believes

Bernie is selling him out on fixed boxing matches, skewing the odds against him by letting other gamblers in on the fact that the bouts are a "sure thing." Caspar wants Leo's permission (though he claims not to need it) to kill Bernie, who pays Leo for protection. "I'm talkin' about friendship," Caspar whines. "I'm talkin' about character. I'm talkin' about—hell, Leo, I ain't embarrassed to use the word—I'm talkin' about ethics."

We soon learn that Leo is reluctant to order a hit on Bernie because he's in love with Bernie's sister, Verna (Marcia Gay Harden). Leo's refusal to whack Bernie, along with his belittling words to Caspar—"You're exactly as big as I let you be and no bigger, and don't forget it. Ever"—clearly are the start of a feud.

After Caspar leaves snarling in a huff, followed closely by his main thug, the murderous Eddie "The Dane" Dane (J. E. Freeman), Tom tells Leo that he's making a mistake by protecting Bernie. Tom fears that his refusal to give up "the sheeny" is sure to start a gang war—a prescient warning, as it turns out.

Here we learn a bit more about Tom. He is deeply in debt to another bookie named Lazarre for a streak of losing bets on horses. Leo offers to clear Tom's debt to Lazarre, but Tom refuses his help. It's a matter of principle. Tom's debts are his own, and he doesn't want to be beholden to Leo, swapping one debt for another. His sins are his alone, and he's prepared to bear them, whatever the cost.

Tom is also a heavy drinker. In the next scene, he is passed out at the Shenandoah Club, a private speakeasy run by Leo. Awakened by the bartender Tad (Olek Krupa), Tom is missing his hat, which Tad reminds him that he lost the night before in a poker game—either to Verna, the love interest of both Tom and Leo, or Mink (Steve

Buscemi), a nervous, minor criminal who is the Dane's "amigo" (gay lover).

Tom goes looking for his hat, his intellectual body armor, at Verna's apartment, and the two verbally spar before falling into bed. Deception abounds, and nothing is quite what it seems. Later that night at Tom's apartment, while Verna sleeps in Tom's bed, Leo shows up in the wee hours, asking Tom to help locate her—Leo has no idea that Verna is asleep in the next room. He's put a tail on Verna in the form of Rug Daniels (Salvatore H. Tornabene), a toupee-clad thug (and the corrupt mayor's aide), but he turns up dead in an alley the next morning. Leo attributes Rug's murder to Caspar, but Tom privately suspects Verna. It's one more piece of information that Tom weighs judiciously and tucks under his hat, which he's reclaimed from Verna.

A day or two later, while heavily drunk, Tom confronts Verna in the women's powder room at the Shenandoah. Brutal verbal fisti-cuffs ensue when Tom says he wants her to stop seeing Leo. She slugs him, and he throws a glass of whiskey at her head, narrowly missing and cracking a large mirror behind her instead.

Back at his apartment, Tom encounters Bernie, who has let him-self in and is seated in one of Tom's armchairs, an ominous grin on his face. In exchange for friendship (and continued protection), Bernie offers to fix a fight for Tom, to help him settle his debt to Lazarre. "I got that crazy dago mad at me," Bernie says. "Don't ask me why. I'm just a small-timer trying to get by like everyone else. I need help from my friends like Leo and you." On the surface, Bernie's words are benign and his presence even somewhat meek, but there's a chillingly sinister undertone to everything he says.

Next, Tom is summoned by Caspar, who also offers to square

Tom's debt with Lazarre if he'll tell him where Bernie is and put a word in with Leo on his behalf. Tom says he'll think about it, and then gets a beating from Caspar's lackeys—Frankie (Mike Starr) and Tic-Tac (Al Mancini)—that knocks his hat off his head. Tom then goes to see Verna at her apartment and tells her that Rug is dead and he thinks she killed him. "You think I murdered someone? Come on, Tom. You know me a little," she says. "Nobody knows anybody—not that well," he replies.

Verna goads him about his feelings for her, asking him to admit that he doesn't want her to see Leo anymore because he's jealous. "Admit that you've got a heart, even though it may be small and feeble, and you can't remember the last time you used it," she says. "If I'd known we were gonna cast our feelings into words, I'd have memorized the Song of Solomon," he retorts snarkily. "Maybe that's why I like you, Tom," she says. "I never met anybody that made being a son of a bitch such a point of pride."

The gangland war is in full swing, played out most spectacularly in the attempted assassination of Leo at his mansion by Caspar's henchmen. Leo survives and meets with Tom in his office above the Shenandoah, where he tells Tom that he's asked Verna to marry him. In turn, Tom tells Leo about his affair with her. Furious, Leo brutally beats Tom, and one of the blows knocks Tom's hat off. As Leo continues the attack, Tom never attempts to retaliate—clambering after his hat instead.

Tom winds up in bed with Verna again after she tells him Leo has broken things off with her. She wakes to Tom smoking (and brooding) on the edge of the bed. He's thinking about a dream he once had, he tells her. "I was walking in the woods. I don't know why. Wind came whippin'. Blew me hat off," he says. "And you chased it, right? You ran and ran. You finally caught up to it. And you picked it up, but it wasn't a hat anymore. It had changed into something else, something wonderful," she says, clearly thinking Tom has finally given her a glimpse of the inner world of his mind. "No, it stayed a hat," he says, nonplussed. "And no, I didn't chase it. Nothing more foolish than a man chasin' his hat."

Tom goes to see Caspar and accepts his offer to turn on Leo and join Caspar's crew. Whether Tom really switches allegiances from Leo to Caspar, or is just posing as a turncoat in order to undermine Caspar's power play, remains to be seen. Still, Tom tells Caspar where he can find Bernie. The Dane, Frankie, and Tic-Tac collect Bernie and take him, with Tom, to Miller's Crossing, a stand of tall trees — the same, we presume, that we saw at the beginning of the film — where a black fedora tumbled through the trees, blown by the wind. The Dane tells Tom that Caspar wants him to be the one who kills Bernie, in order to prove his allegiance. In the film's most compelling scene, Tom drags a sniveling Bernie to an opening in the trees, draws his gun, and trains it at Bernie's head. Bernie falls to his knees, begging for his life, utterly humiliated:

Tommy, you can't do this. You don't bump guys. You're not like those animals back there. It's not right, Tom. They can't make us do this. It's a wrong situation. They can't make us different people than we are. We're not muscle. I never killed anybody. I used a little information for a chisel, that's all. It's my nature, Tom. I can't help it. Somebody hands me an angle, I play it. I don't deserve to die for that. Do you think I do? But I tell you what — I never crossed a friend. I never killed anybody, I never crossed a friend. We're not like those animals. This is not us. It's a dream, Tommy! I'm praying to you! I can't die. I can't die out here in the woods like a dumb animal. In the woods like a dumb animal! Like a, like a dumb animal! I can't—I can't—I can't die out here in the woods like a dumb animal. I can't die! I'm praying to you. Look in your heart.

The gun fires. For a moment, we think Tom has killed Bernie, but instead, he's fired past him, sparing his life. Tom has looked in his heart and found compassion. He tells Bernie to run, to disappear, to never show his face in town again, or else he really will kill him. Back in town, one of Leo's heavies, Terry, finds Tom, punches him (knocking off his hat, which he then brushes off and hands back to him), and says he's come to deliver a warning from Leo, who believes Tom really has double-crossed him and aligned himself with Caspar. "Tell Leo he's not God on the throne," Tom says defiantly. "He's just a cheap political boss with more hair tonic than brains." Tom meets with Caspar, who informs him that Mink has disappeared. Meanwhile, the Dane visits Verna, and after killing the two heavies Leo had sent to protect her, tells her that Tom has murdered Bernie, who in the next scene shows up at Tom's place to blackmail him.

The Dane then comes calling, suspecting that Tom has spared Bernie's life and betrayed Caspar. Accompanied by Frankie and Tic-Tac, he muscles Tom into the car and drives him out to Miller's Crossing to find Bernie's body, which the audience knows isn't there. Tom is characteristically stoic as he marches to what will surely be his own demise. Finally, the pressure catches up with him and he doubles over next to a tree—his hat tumbling off his head—and retches. He marches on, stumbling, toward the clearing where Bernie's body should be but isn't. Just as the Dane is about to shoot Tom, Frankie and Tic-Tac discover a decomposing body. The corpse has been shot in the face, disguising its true identity. But Caspar's men believe it to be Bernie. (Later we learn that it's Mink, whom Bernie had murdered and left in the crossing, and that Mink—not Verna—had killed Rug in some kind of mix-up.)

Tom goes to Caspar, hoping to convince him that the Dane is a turncoat and is using Bernie as the scapegoat. Essentially confessing that he has not followed orders to murder Bernie, Tom tells Caspar that Bernie will be at his apartment—the Barton Arms—that night. (When Joel and Ethan Coen were writing their ambitiously complex screenplay for *Miller's Crossing*, they famously came to an impasse in the plot. Though they've adamantly claimed they weren't suffering from writer's block, the Coens took a break from writing what they had tentatively titled *The Bighead* to visit friends in Los Angeles, where they consumed copious amounts of coffee and do-nuts and watched cheesy films such as the Diane Keaton romantic comedy *Baby Boom*. It was during this hiatus that brothers came up with the idea for their next film—*Barton Fink*, the story of a Jewish New York playwright who comes to Hollywood to write for a movie studio and suffers from near-fatal writer's block. The Coens returned to New York and wrote *Barton Fink* in just a few weeks and then returned to *Miller's Crossing*, finishing the screenplay.)

When the Dane comes to tell Caspar that Mink is dead, Caspar accuses the Dane of betrayal and shoots him dead. On the rainy street outside Caspar's lair, Verna confronts Tom with a gun, threatening to kill him for murdering Bernie. Tom tells her that Bernie is still alive. With the gun pressed to Tom's chin, Verna hesitates. She doesn't have it in her to pull the trigger. "It isn't easy, is it Verna?" he taunts, as she runs away weeping.

Back at the Barton Arms, Caspar has arrived to kill Bernie.

Bernie, however, hides in the hallway outside Tom's apartment, catches Caspar by surprise, and kills him. Tom arrives on the scene and double-crosses Bernie, taking a roll of cash from Caspar's pocket and the gun from his dead hand. He aims at Bernie, who drops to his knees in a repeat of the scene from Miller's Crossing. "Tommy, look in your heart," he begs. "What heart?" Tom replies and pulls the trigger.

Bernie Bernbaum is a fascinating character, the first explicitly Jewish character the Coen brothers created for the screen. He possesses all of the negative anti-Semitic stereotypes of classical depictions of Jews. A modern-day Shylok, he is sneaky, untrustworthy, and motivated largely by lust for money. Throughout the film, racial and ethnic slurs are bandied about with abandon, particularly when it comes to Bernie, who is called, variously, "the shmatte kid," "the sheeny," and a "Hebrew." ("What's one Hebrew more or less?" Tom says to Leo after Caspar first asks to have the bookie bumped off.)

The Coens are Jewish, but seem to be comfortable employing the ethnic prejudices that would have been commonplace in the 1920s, in order to advance their plot. While religion is never explicitly addressed in the film, it contains a religious subtext. The Irish and Italian gangsters share a common Roman Catholic tradition, if not faith, and it would have been scandalous at the time for a Catholic to marry a Jew, as Leo plans to wed Verna.

Tom uses the money he takes from Caspar's corpse to square his debts with Lazarre, and then places another bet. A few days later, in the final scene of the film, Tom turns up in the woods—a location that looks a lot like the crossing—for Bernie's burial. Apart from a rabbi, who reads a prayer over the grave, the only people in attendance are Verna and Leo, who is wearing a yarmulke.

"Big turnout," Tom says mockingly to Verna, who tells him to "drop dead," before getting into Leo's chauffeur-driven car and driving away, leaving Tom and Leo alone. Leo pleads with Tom to come back to work for him, saying that he wished Tom had told him about his scheme to double-cross Caspar. Leo really believed that Tom had betrayed him, but now he knows now it was all a hoax. He says that he and Verna, who proposed to him this time, are going to get married. "I forgive you," Leo says about Tom's affair with Verna. "I didn't ask for that, and I don't want it," Tom snaps. "Good-bye, Leo."

The film ends with a tight shot on Tom's face as he watches, wistfully, Leo walking away. Tom adjusts his hat, pulling the brim down tightly over his eyes, and the credits roll.

THE MORAL OF THE STORY . . .

Throughout the film, Tom's loyalty has been to Leo, the Lion, the *pater familias*. It's never clear why this is, though some critics have speculated that Tom is in love with Leo and that his affair with Verna is a way of getting close to the man he loves. Homosexuality surely is a subtext in the Coens' most complicated plot, but I think romantic love is too simplistic an explanation for Tom's undying devotion to Leo. Who knows what the backstory between the two men really is? Perhaps Leo brought Tom from Ireland to the United States, to give him a better life. Maybe Leo reminds Tom of his own father, or the father he never had. Whatever the explanation, when it comes to Leo, Tom is ruled by his heart, which terrifies him. Tom is, above all, a reasonable man, and when he allows compassion to rule his head in sparing Bernie, the consequences are disastrous.

Perhaps it is better — safer, at least — for Tom to remain ensconced in the world of his mind, with all of his emotions and wounds hidden safely under his hat. He remains in the woods, where at one point it seemed that God had intervened to save him by producing a body that wasn't supposed to be there. Just as some observant Jewish men keep their heads covered by a hat or a yarmulke as a sign of their respect and deference in the presence of God (who is always present), Tom's hat may be a symbol of his reverence for the Almighty in some fashion.

The Coens have been asked many times about the significance of the hat in *Miller's Crossing*. The brothers based their film in large part on Dashiell Hammett's hard-boiled *The Glass Key*, borrowing some plot points, characters, and even dialogue directly from the 1931 detective novel. In Hammett's book, the hero, Ned Beaumont (a political fixer), asks about a missing hat. When another character asks him why he's so interested in the hat, Beaumont says, "I don't know. I'm only an amateur detective, but it looks like a thing that might have some meaning, one way or another."[4]

While admitting that they began the screenplay with the simple idea of a hat blowing through the woods, the Coens, in their typically oblique way, have declined to reveal its intended meaning, even to Gabriel Byrne, who played Tom himself. In an interview after the release of the film in 1990, Byrne said, "It was really weird that nobody mentioned the hat all the way through the movie. I said to Joel at one point, 'What is the significance of the hat? Is the hat significant?' And he said, 'Mmmm hmmm.' And that was it."[5]

BARTON FINK

CHAPTER 4

BARTON FINK

"I'll show you the life of the mind!"

THE FOREST

In 1941 New York City, Barton Fink is the latest toast of Broadway, who, unfortunately, believes his own reviews. Champion (in his own mind) of the working class, Fink wants to bring his "Theater of the Common Man" to an even wider audience than the Great White Way. Hoping to finance his heart's work with a lucrative short-term contract working for "the man," Fink accepts a position as a staff writer for a Hollywood movie studio and ends up being assigned to write a B movie about wrestling. In Los Angeles, Fink checks into the hellish Hotel Earle, with its infernal heat and melting wallpaper, where he immediately is felled by stultifying writer's block. He turns for help to his neighbor, traveling insurance salesman Charlie Meadows, alcoholic novelist-turned-studio-hack William Mayhew, and Mayhew's mistress (and ghostwriter) Audrey, who winds up dead in bed next to Fink after the two share a night of passion. Paralyzed by self-doubt, Fink turns to Meadows for help in dealing with what he believes is his crime, but he soon realizes Meadows is a psychopathic serial killer and not the Everyman of Fink's imagination.

THE TREES

A few years ago, while visiting a college friend in northern California who had recently become a Buddhist, I spent some time at the San Francisco Zen Center where she is a lay practitioner. Her task on that particular day was to sound a huge wooden gong outside the meditation room where several dozen lay and monastic Zen practitioners had gathered for *zazen*, or meditation. Each sounding of the gong indicated a transition in the zazen, as those meditating strove to center themselves, calming their minds and letting thoughts drift through their consciousness without fixating on them.

For me, a sometimes churchgoing Catholic-turned-Baptist-turned-freelance Episcopalian, observing the zazen was a fascinating experience. I felt drawn to the peace and tranquility their meditation seemed to foster. On our way out of the afternoon session, we stopped in the Zen Center's bookstore and I bought a small laminated sign on a silk cord that says in black calligraphic script, "Don't believe everything you think." It hangs on the doorknob of the room at home where I do most of my writing. It is a subtle reminder that I create best when I am centered, but I also like to think of it as a kind of cautionary road sign along life's journey in general: Beware the life of the mind!

"Don't believe everything you think" would have been the perfect tagline for the Coen brothers' 1991 film *Barton Fink*. Set in Los Angeles in 1941 around the time of the Japanese attacks on Pearl Harbor, *Barton Fink* is the story of a successful New York playwright — the eponymous Mr. Fink (played by John Turturro) — who begrudgingly agrees to what he thinks will be a short tenure as a Hollywood screenwriter for one of the big movie studios to finance his "real" art — "the creation of a new, living theater of, about, and for the common man."

Hollywood comes calling when Fink becomes the toast of Broadway with his play *Bare Ruined Choirs: Triumph of the Common Man*, a terribly earnest, thinly veiled chronicle of his own life as part of a struggling family of Jewish fishmongers on New York City's Lower East Side. As the laudatory reviews flood in, Fink's agent, Garland (David Warrilow), convinces the intellectual dramaturge that he should jump at the chance to go to Los Angeles to write for "the pictures." "A brief tenure in Hollywood could support you through the writing of any number of plays," he says.

Fink arrives in Los Angeles with two pieces of luggage — a small suitcase and his Underwood typewriter — and checks into the less-than-stellar Hotel Earle, a faded art deco affair that he has chosen in lieu of one of Beverly Hills' finest hotels, where the studio would have gladly housed him. Here on the outskirts of town, Fink believes he'll be closer to the common man, the *real* Los Angelinos. The empty lobby of the Earle — whose motto is "for a day or a lifetime" — is dusty, dark, and oppressive, lit by shafts of amber light and ventilated by slow-moving fans that seem to be more for appearance than anything else.

After arriving at the front desk and sounding a bell that seems to ring for a preternaturally long time, a bellhop (Steve Buscemi) appears from a door in the floor carrying a lone shoe, his hands covered in shoe polish. He introduces himself as Chet, or CHET! as he writes on a scrap of paper, and asks whether Fink is a "tranz or a rez."* They determine that Fink, who intends to stay for an unspecified length

*Tranz = transient; rez = resident.

of time, is a "rez," and he's transported to his room on the sixth floor by a cadaverous elevator operator named Pete, whose only words are, "Next stop: six" and "This stop: six."

The ancient elevator deposits Fink, already sweating, into a long, narrow hallway with high ceilings and faded palm tree wallpaper where every door looks the same but for a different pair of men's shoes waiting neatly on the floor outside. (Chet explains that one of the perks at the Earle is a complimentary shoeshine every day.) Fink's room is cramped and tired, sparsely decorated with a writing desk, a creaky metal bed, and a framed print of a bathing suit–clad young woman who is gazing at a sparkling ocean. The profusely sweating Fink manages to pry open one of the windows a few inches, only to discover that it looks out on nothing in particular.

Asked about the choice of setting for *Barton Fink*, Joel Coen explained, "Ethan always describes most hotels as ghost ships where one notes signs of the presence of other passengers without ever seeing them. The sole indication [at the Hotel Earle] is the shoes in the corridors. One imagines it peopled by unsuccessful traveling salesmen with sad sexual lives and who cry alone in their rooms."[6] The Coens found their inspiration for the Hotel Earle in Austin, Texas, while filming *Blood Simple* a few years earlier. Across the street was a sinister-looking hotel whose stationery bore the slogan "The Hotel for a Day or a Lifetime."[7] The Coens, in *Barton Fink*, wanted to make the Earle feel like the strangest hotel in the world.[8]

When Fink goes to bed his first night at the Earle, he notices a stain on the ceiling above the bed, sees that the wallpaper is buckled in places, and hears a mosquito buzzing. The next morning, as he sets out for the movie studio to meet his new boss, he is anything but rested and his face is spotted with mosquito bites. (Later in the film,

Ben Geisler [Tony Shalhoub], a brusque movie producer, tells Fink that there are no mosquitoes in Los Angeles because mosquitoes breed in humid, swampy conditions and Los Angeles is a desert.)

In a scene repeated in many of the Coen brothers' films — in the back room of a bar in *Blood Simple*, on the 45th floor of a high-rise office building in *The Hudsucker Proxy*, and in a palatial home office in *The Big Lebowski* — across an expansive desk, Fink, the antihero, meets the corpulent, corrupt man who symbolizes absolute power in his world. In this case, it's the studio head Jack Lipnik (Michael Lerner). When Lipnik, an abrasive, bombastic egoist based in part on the real-life movie mogul Louis B. Mayer, asks Fink what kind of movies he likes, Fink admits that he doesn't go to the pictures very often.

Lipnik responds in machine-gun staccato:

That's OK, that's OK, that's OK — that's just fine. You probably walked in here thinking that was going to be a handicap, thinking we wanted people who knew something about the medium, maybe even thinking there was all kind of technical mumbo-jumbo to learn. You were dead wrong. We're only interested in one thing: Can you tell a story, Bart? Can you make us laugh, can you make us cry, can you make us wanna break out in joyous song? Is that more than one thing? OK. The point is, I run this dump, and I don't know the technical mumbo-jumbo. Why do I run it? I've got horse sense, g–dd–it. Showmanship. And also, and I hope Lou told you this, I am bigger and meaner than any kike in this town. Did you tell him that, Lou? And I don't mean my dick's bigger than yours, it's not a sexual thing — although you're the writer, you would know more about that. Coffee?

Because Fink doesn't express a preference for any particular film genre and because, as Lipnik explains, his street sense makes him ill-suited to write biblical epics, Westerns, or pirate films—Fink is assigned to a Wallace Beery wrestling film, a B movie if there ever was one, and the farthest thing from Fink's high-minded proletarian plays about the struggles of the common man. Fink is flummoxed —and terrified—by his assignment.

Before dispatching Fink back to the Earle to get started, Lipnik, speaking to his toady assistant, Lou (Jon Polito), says, "Ah, hell, let Bart take a crack at it. He'll get into the swing of things or I don't know writers.... Bart, keep it simple. We don't gotta tackle the world our first time out. The important thing is we all have that Barton Fink feeling, but since you're Barton Fink I'm assuming you have it in spades. Seriously Bart, I like you. We're off to a good start. D–mit, if all our writers were like you I wouldn't have to get so g–dd–n involved. I'd like to see something by the end of the week."

Almost immediately, Fink is assailed by writer's block. Back at the hotel, he sits down at the writing desk, puts a sheet of paper in the Underwood, and pounds out the first lines of his screenplay:

FADE IN: A tenement building on Manhattan's Lower East Side. Early morning traffic is audible. As is ...

Fink stops typing and listens. We hear the sounds of manic laughter mixed with sobs. It's a man's voice coming from the room next door. After a few moments, Fink picks up the phone and calls Chet to complain that the noise is bothering him. A moment later, he hears the phone ring in the room next door and a man's voice saying, "Who?" followed by pounding footsteps and a knock at his door. Quaking and sweating, Fink timidly opens the door to see Charlie Meadows (John Goodman)—easily a head taller and twice his weight—filling the doorway with his barely contained hostility.

Charlie asks Fink if he's the one who complained, and, stammering, Fink says he called downstairs because he was afraid someone might be in distress. This seems to placate Charlie, whose demeanor changes quickly to one of supplicant, begging his neighbor's forgiveness for disturbing him and inviting Fink for a drink. He introduces himself and asks Fink what he does, to which Fink responds, "Well, I'm a writer actually."

Charlie is a traveling insurance salesman. "You might say I sell peace of mind," he says. "Fire, theft, and casualty are not things that only happen to other people—that's what I tell 'em." (Little does Fink know that all three are about to happen to him.)

The conversation continues:

Barton: "Strange as it may seem, Charlie, I guess I write about people like you. The average working stiff. The common man."

Charlie: "Well ain't that a kick in the head!"

Barton: "Yeah, I guess it is. But in a way, that's exactly the point. There's a few people in New York—hopefully our numbers are growing—who feel we have an opportunity now to forge something real out of everyday experience, create a theater for the masses that's based on a few simple truths—not on some shopworn abstractions about drama that don't hold true today, if they ever did."

(He gazes at Charlie.)

"I don't guess this means much to you."

Charlie: "Hell, I could tell you some stories—"

Barton: "And that's the point, that we all have stories. The hopes and dreams of the common man are as noble as those of any king. It's the stuff of life—why shouldn't it be the stuff of theater? G–dd–it. Why should that be a hard pill to swallow? Don't call it new theater, Charlie; call it real theater. Call it our theater."

Charlie: "I can see you feel pretty strongly about it."

Barton: "Well, I don't mean to get up on my high horse, but why shouldn't we look at ourselves up there? Who cares about the Fifth Earl of Bastrop and Lady Higginbottom and … and … and who killed Nigel Grinch-Gibbons?"

Charlie: "I can feel my butt getting sore already."

Barton: "Exactly, Charlie! You understand what I'm saying—a lot more than some of these literary types. Because you're a real man!"

Charlie: "And I could tell you some stories—"

Barton: "Sure you could! And yet many writers do everything in their power to insulate themselves from the common man—from where they live, from where they trade, from where they fight and love and converse and … and … and … so naturally their work suffers, and regresses into empty formalism and—well, I'm spouting off again, but to put it in your language, the theater becomes as phony as a three-dollar bill."

The next day at the studio, Fink continues to try to find guidance about how he should write the wrestling film. The film's producer, Ben Geisler, is no help but suggests that Fink find a more veteran writer at the studio to mentor him. A few minutes later, while in the men's room, Fink meets his new mentor, the renowned Southern novelist W. P. "Bill" Mayhew (John Mahoney), a bourbon-swilling, seersucker-wearing gentleman clearly patterned after William Faulkner, who did, in fact, spend time in Hollywood writing for films (including a Wallace Beery wrestling picture called *Flesh*).

Mayhew invites Fink to his writer's bungalow, where a sign announces he is working on a film called *Slave Ship*. But when Fink turns up, he's greeted instead by Mayhew's loyal assistant (and mistress) Audrey (Judy Davis) who explains, while Mayhew whoops and hollers like a banshee in the background, that he is "indisposed." "When he can't write, he drinks," she says. "Please don't judge us."

By the time Fink returns to the Earle, where the wallpaper has again been peeling away from the walls, melting in the heat and oozing puslike glue, the psychic static interfering with his creative flow has reached a fever pitch. He's relieved when Charlie stops by for a visit.

"You know, in a way, I envy you, Charlie," Fink says. "Your daily routine—you know what's expected. You know the drill. My job is to plumb the depths, so to speak, dredge something up from inside, something honest. There's no road map for that territory and exploring it can be painful. The kind of pain most people don't know anything about."

Fink, the self-styled Everyman who is, in reality, a cultural elitist, says this without any hint of irony, without a whiff of empathy for what Charlie—the authentic "common man" he heard moaning and weeping before they ever met—might be suffering. It never crosses Fink's mind that his neighbor's pain, whether emotional or spiritual, might be more important than his own "noble" writing process.

Meanwhile, the lines between fantasy and reality and between sleep and waking life begin to blur as Fink gets to know his mentor Mayhew, who turns out to be not just an alcoholic, but an abusive one. Fink falls for Audrey, who later reveals she is Mayhew's ghostwriter and has been for some time. Simultaneously, Fink comes face-to-face with the realization that the filmmaking world is based solely on "the worship of Mammon" (as Mayhew puts it)—an immoral, arbitrary universe ruled by the whims of its cruel despot, Lipnik.

Back at the Hotel Earle, Fink faces a deadline with the despot and is paralyzed by his thoughts. He stares blankly at the page in his typewriter, sweating in panic, as the hotel room slowly disintegrates around him. He calls Audrey for help, and when she arrives, the two spend a passionate night together. "We all need understanding, Barton. Even you — tonight — it's all you really need," she says.

In the morning, Fink awakes to find Audrey lying beside him, naked. He swats at a mosquito on her shoulder, squishing it into a bloody bruise, but Audrey doesn't move, and it's then he notices the enormous bloodstain seeping from her body onto the mattress. Fink turns her over and discovers a fatal stab wound. In a panic, fearing that he killed her in his sleep, Fink turns to Charlie for help, who disposes of the body.

Fink makes it to his poolside meeting at Lipnik's Beverly Hills estate, where he is supposed to summarize the basic plot of the Wallace Beery wrestling picture. He gets as far as his opening setting — a tenement building on the Lower East Side — and says he prefers not to reveal any more for fear of corrupting the creative process. Lipnik's toady assistant, Lou (John Polito), chastises Fink, telling him "right now the contents of your head are the property of Capitol Pictures." Lipnik proceeds to turn on Lou, firing him before literally kissing Fink's feet and sending him back to the Earle to finish his masterpiece.

Charlie appears at Fink's door with a medium-sized box containing, he says, some personal effects and asks him to hold on to it for him since he has to get out of town for a few days. "Maybe it'll bring you good luck," Charlie says. "Yeah, it'll help you finish your script." Fink puts the box on his desk and resumes his catatonic position in front of the typewriter. He interrupts his stupor by opening the desk drawer and pulling out a Gideon Bible. He turns randomly to the middle of the Hebrew Scriptures, and the camera pans down to the book of Daniel, chapter 2, verse 5.

> *5And the king, Nebuchadnezzar, answered and said to the Chaldeans, I recall not my dream; if ye will not make known unto me my dream, and its interpretation, ye shall be cut in pieces, and your tents shall be made a dunghill.*

Fink flips to the beginning of the Scriptures, to the first verse of the first chapter of the book of Genesis, where the traditional text has been replaced with:

> *1Fade in on a tenement building on Manhattan's Lower East Side. Faint traffic noise is audible;*
> *2As is the cry of the fishmongers.*
> *3And God said, Let there be light: and there was light.*

In the Bible, King Nebuchadnezzar of Babylon is a terrorist and a tyrant known for his love of gruesome torture. Nebuchadnezzar forced Zedekiah, king of Judah, to watch each of his sons be killed just before his own eyes were gouged out, ensuring that the horrible image of his dead offspring would be the last thing Zedekiah ever witnessed. Nebuchadnezzar was also the one who threw Shadrach, Meshach, and Abednego into a raging fire from which they were saved by an angel—an act of divine intervention that eventually led to Nebuchadnezzar's conversion.

In the passage that Fink reads, the Babylonian king is tormented by nightmares that he doesn't understand. He summons all his regular soothsayers and advisers to tell him not only what his dreams meant but what they were—an impossible task. If Nebuchadnezzar's advisers fail to read his mind, he'll have them cut into pieces, and their homes and families destroyed for good measure.

A phone call interrupts Fink's impromptu and stress-filled Bible study. It's from Chet telling him that two Los Angeles Police detectives want to see him in the lobby. In the elevator on the way downstairs, an increasingly haggard Fink has a conversation with Pete, who looks even more cadaverous than usual in his role as a modern-day Phlegyas, the boatman on the river Styx who ferried Dante and Virgil across the river Styx from Earth to Hades in Dante's *Inferno* (aka *Divine Comedy*).

Barton: "You read the Bible, Pete?"

Pete: "The Holy Bible?"

Barton: "Yeah."

Pete: "Yeah, I think so. Anyway, I've heard about it."

In the lobby, the detectives tell Fink that Charlie Meadows isn't a sad-sack traveling salesman but is actually the serial killer Karl "Madman" Mundt, who is known for taking a shotgun to his victims before he decapitates them.

Back in his room, sitting once again, sweating in stunned silence in front of the Underwood, Fink begins to write. He works all night and finishes the script for the Wallace Beery wrestling picture, stopping to call his agent, Garland, back in New York to say it's the best work he's ever done. To celebrate his accomplishment, Fink heads out to the local USO hall, where he dances wildly with a pretty woman in a red dress. When a sailor who is shipping out the next day asks to cut in, Fink refuses. A fight ensues, with Fink—oblivious to any reality outside his own mind—screaming at his military attackers, "I'm a writer, you monsters! I create. I create for a living. I'm a creator!" Pointing to his head, he yells, "This is my uniform. This is how I serve the common man!"

When Fink returns to his room at the Earle, he finds the two detectives in his room reading the screenplay he'd finished a few hours before. As they handcuff him to the bed, they tell him Mundt has killed Audrey and Mayhew and that they think Fink is his accomplice. The hotel room is even hotter than before, with sheets of soiled wallpaper falling away from the walls like banana peels. "Charlie's back," Fink moans. "It's hot. He's back."

The detectives step into the hallway, where the heat is so intense you can almost see it coming off the floor in waves. Flames shoot out of the elevator shaft, and the cops shout for Mundt to show himself. Charlie steps out of the flames and smoke to face them down the corridor. He puts his insurance policy case on the ground, pulls out a shotgun, and shoots one of the detectives, then begins to run toward the other, shouting, "Look upon me! Look upon me! I'll show you the life of the mind!" He overtakes the remaining detective, puts the shotgun to his forehead, and fires.

Face-to-face with Fink inside his hotel room, Charlie explains why he kills people: "Most guys I just feel sorry for. Yeah. It tears me up inside, to think about what they're going through. How trapped they are. I understand it. I feel for 'em. So I try and help them out. Jesus. Yeah. I know what it feels like, when things get all balled up at the head office. It puts you through hell, Barton. So I help people out. I just wish someone would do as much for me."

When Fink asks Charlie, "Why me?" Charlie screams at him, "Because you don't listen!... C'mon Barton, you think you know about pain? You think I made your life hell? You're just a tourist with a typewriter. Barton, I live here." Charlie then kneels down next to the bed and, with monstrous strength, bends the bars, freeing Fink from his shackles, before calmly walking into the flaming hallway, opening the door to his room, and stepping through the fire. Fink puts on his coat and hat, grabs the box and his script, and walks out of the Earle for the last time.

When he meets with Lipnik to present the screenplay he thinks is his best work ever, the movie mogul tells him it's terrible and that he needs to be put in his place. "They don't want to see a guy wrestling with his soul!" he shouts. "We don't put Wally Beery in some fruity movie about suffering!"

Lipnik sentences Fink to the Sisyphean fate of indentured servitude at the studio. "You're under contract and you're gonna stay that way," Lipnik roars. "Anything you write will be the property of Capitol Pictures. And Capitol Pictures will not produce anything you write. Not until you grow up a little. You ain't no writer, Fink — you're a g–dd–n write-off!"

The film ends with a shell-shocked Fink sitting on a beach, with the box (possibly containing Audrey's head, we realize) next to him on the sand. A beautiful young woman who looks exactly like the bathing beauty from the picture in his hotel room walks toward him and sits down.

"You're very beautiful. Are you in pictures?" he says.

"Don't be silly," she answers, before turning to look at the surf, lifting a hand to shield her eyes. A bird flies into the frame and dives into the water — and the screen goes blank.

The viewer is left to wonder whether the whole episode in Los Angeles was a dream — a mere figment of Fink's imagination and a projection of his greatest fears about himself.

THE MORAL OF THE STORY ...

Unlike many other mystical traditions, Zen Buddhism maintains that we can know reality. It's not hidden. It's not something we have to wait until the next life in order to grasp fully. The mystery of reality is present in the wind that blows, in the blades of grass beneath our feet, in the sunlight on our faces. But we have to be awake—watchful and open—to see it. We can be blinded by our own thought life so much so that we miss what's real and right in front of us.

In that spirit, *Barton Fink* is a cautionary tale about the dangers of living in our imaginations. When we begin to believe not only our own reviews but also our every thought, we can end up creating and living in our own private hells.

THE HUDSUCKER PROXY

CHAPTER 5

THE HUDSUCKER PROXY

*"I'm never supposed to do this,
but do you have a better idea?"*

THE FOREST

Waring Hudsucker, the cherubic president of Hudsucker Industries in 1958 New York City, receives perhaps the best quarterly report his company has ever had and promptly throws himself through the window of his high-rise boardroom. Rather than see this for the tragedy that it is, his partner, Sidney Mussburger, seizes it as an opportunity to make even more money by replacing Hudsucker with a patsy.

He finds that patsy in the hayseed naïf Norville Barnes, fresh off the bus from Muncie, Indiana, where he has just graduated with a degree in business. Barnes, whose brilliant business plan involves marketing the hula hoop, becomes the toast of the town, but Amy Archer, the fast-talking Pulitzer Prize–winning investigative reporter, suspects Barnes to be the fraud he really is. But her investigation leads to surprising results. She falls for Barnes, who follows his predecessor out the 44th-floor boardroom window, only to be saved by divine intervention.

THE TREES

Tibetan Buddhists call it the *bhavacakra*. It is the Wheel of Life, or Wheel of Becoming, an artistic depiction of *samsara*—the continuous cycle of life, death, and reincarnation—in the form of a circle. The wheel usually has six spokes, each representing different qualities or stages of unenlightened existence. Throughout a life or different lives—karmic cycles—a soul moves outward from earthbound, unenlightened existence toward spiritual enlightenment.

The Hudsucker Proxy is a kind of modern, animated bhavacakra, tracing the path of its two-dimensional, cartoonish human characters as they pass through cyclical trials and tribulations to attain a modicum of enlightenment, but with a decidedly un-Buddhist twist: divine intervention.

The film opens on a snowy night in New York City, 1958. It's New Year's Eve, a narrator's voice tells us, and Norville Barnes (Tim Robbins), our antihero, is standing on a ledge outside the president's office of the Hudsucker Industries skyscraper. "Over in the Waldorf the big shots is dancin' to the strains of Guy Lombardo," the narrator tells us. "Down in Times Square the little folks is a-watchin' and a-waitin' fo' that big ball to drop. They all tryin' to catch holt a one moment of time to be able to say, 'Right now! This is it! I got it!' Course by then it'll be past. But they all happy, evvybody havin' a good time. Well, almost evvybody. They's a few lost souls floatin' 'round out there."

Barnes is one of those lost souls, perched terrified above Madison

Avenue and about to hurl himself down forty-four floors to the sidewalk. The narrator—the omniscient voice of God perhaps—begins to tell us Barnes's story, but for that, he has to go back in time a month or so to the antihero's arrival in the big-city rat race from the most middle-American of places: Muncie, Indiana.

A wide-eyed, fresh-faced hayseed, Barnes disembarks the bus from Muncie carrying a small suitcase emblazoned with a sticker from the Muncie School of Business Administration, from which he's recently matriculated. He walks to an employment agency and stands outside with a group of other job seekers watching an enormous flip board advertising openings for pastry chef, steamfitter, grave digger, cantor (reform), linotype man, and so on. When a listing for "business executive" appears, Barnes is momentarily heartened until he reads the fine print: "experience needed." Dejected, he walks away.

The camera jumps to the inside of a cavernous executive boardroom where dozens of nondescript, graying men line an absurdly long meeting table overlooking the tops of New York City's many skyscrapers. At the head of the table sits Waring Hudsucker (Charles Durning), smiling weakly in his expensive three-piece suit and winding his silver pocket watch. One of the board members is delivering a quarterly report, outlining the stunning successes of Hudsucker Industries. The camera cuts again to Barnes, seated at the counter of a coffee shop, looking over the newspaper want ads. Each ad lists the one requirement Barnes doesn't possess: experience. He leaves the coffee shop, still dejected. When the waitress buses his dishes, we see that his coffee cup has left a brown stain in the shape of a perfect circle around an ad that reads "THE FUTURE IS NOW. Start building yours at Hudsucker Industries. Low pay. Long hours. No EXPERIENCE NECESSARY."

Again, the camera returns to the Hudsucker boardroom, where the moneyman finishes his stellar report on the company's earnings. "In short, we're loaded," he says. Waring Hudsucker lights a cigar, clears his throat as if to speak, but instead climbs up on the table, takes a running start, and hurls himself through the window, plummeting toward the sidewalk. As Hudsucker leaps to his death, we return to Barnes. The newspaper from the coffee shop blows down the sidewalk and wraps itself around his leg. He picks it up, sees the ad, and heads toward the Hudsucker building. Barnes walks through the door just as Hudsucker, whose last act on earth is to motion for a mother and daughter to get out of the way so he doesn't squish them, lands on the sidewalk, meeting his spectacular demise. In this case, as one man goes out a window, another enters through revolving doors.

While Barnes begins his orientation in the basement mailroom, with a foreman barking instructions that always end with the refrain, "If you don't ..., they dock ya!" We return to the 44th-floor boardroom, where we meet Sid Mussburger (Paul Newman), Hudsucker's right-hand man. Unfazed by the shocking suicide, Mussburger picks up the lit cigar, saying, "Pity to waste a whole Monte Cristo." He immediately turns his attention to the fate of the company, already conspiring about how to spare Hudsucker Industries from the financial fallout of the boss's untimely death. Hudsucker has no family and left no will, we learn, and the company bylaws stipulate that in such an instance Hudsucker's controlling interest in the company be made available to the public within thirty days of his death.

Mussburger continues plotting how the board can maintain control of the company and decides that the only way is to depress the stock value so the board can buy a controlling interest itself. For that, he figures, they will need to find a replacement for Hudsucker—a patsy so incompetent that his appointment will spook the market and send stock prices plummeting.

Back in the mailroom, Barnes is clearly pleased to have his new job, no matter how lousy it is. He whistles while he works, sorting letters into mail slots, until a manager arrives with a dreaded blue letter, an interoffice memo from one executive to another that must be hand-delivered. Blue letters are always bad news, and the messenger is usually shot, metaphorically speaking. Barnes is the only mailroom lackey who hasn't made himself scarce, so the unfortunate task falls to him.

He rides the elevator to the 44th floor to deliver the letter to Mussburger himself. Inside a cavernous, cryptlike office, Mussburger is seated behind a large desk, still smoking the Monte Cristo and talking on the phone about finding his patsy. Though terrified, Barnes musters the gumption to pitch his idea for what he thinks a million-dollar invention. It's a simple circle. "You know, for kids," he says, smiling sheepishly. Mussburger threatens to fire Barnes but realizes that his patsy has presented himself. He gruffly interrogates Barnes about his background, assuming he is just another imbecile from the mailroom. "You weren't blessed with much education were you?" he says. Barnes tells him he's a graduate of the Muncie College of Business Administration. Mussburger counters that he must not have excelled in his studies, but Barnes says he made the dean's list. Mussburger says that his friends probably thought he was a nitwit and a jerk, but Barnes tells him that he was voted "most likely to succeed." With that, Mussburger fires him and tells him to "get out of my sight."

A flummoxed Barnes bobbles the lit cigar in his hand (which

Mussburger had offered him), setting on fire a contract lying on Mussburger's desk—it's the Bumstead contract, a major deal the company's been working on for three years, and in the ensuing chaos Barnes manages to set fire to a nearby trash bin, as well as to the leg of his pants. Trying to make things right, Barnes hurls the flaming trash bin at the window, shattering it, and in the sudden rush of wind that follows, the remaining pages of the contract are sucked out of the office. Mussburger lunges to catch them and tumbles out the broken window, where Barnes catches him by the legs, saving him from certain death. As a reward, or perhaps convinced that Barnes really is a total moron, Mussburger makes him president. A montage shows Barnes's transformation from mailroom lackey to business executive, and the wunderkind quickly becomes the toast of the town, a real "idea man."

Next we meet the staff of the *Manhattan Argus* newspaper assembled in the office of the editor (John Mahoney), who barks orders at the reporters to find the "real" story on the young company president. Enter Amy Archer (Jennifer Jason Leigh), a fast-talking Pulitzer Prize–winning undercover reporter who claims that Barnes is a fraud. Archer promises to infiltrate Hudsucker Industries to get the scoop on him.

Over the next few scenes, Archer begins work as Barnes's secretary, using her position to snoop around Hudsucker Industries. Her unflattering articles about Barnes produce Mussburger's desired results: the stock price plummets. Yet even as she writes her scathing stories, Archer begins to soften toward Barnes.

Barnes is, if maddeningly gullible, a sweet-hearted fellow. At the company Christmas party, Archer finds Barnes standing on a balcony, and just as she's about to confess that she is an imposter, Barnes interrupts her with a monologue on spirituality and the meaning of life. Talking of karma and reincarnation, he rambles on about "the great cycle of life, death, and rebirth." "Yeah, I think I've heard of that—what goes around comes around," replies Archer morosely. "That's it!" Barnes answers cheerfully. "A great wheel that gives us each what we deserve." With renewed confidence, Barnes says he's going to present his big idea—"you know, for kids!"—to the board the next day.

The camera jumps to the boardroom, where Barnes is demonstrating his great invention: a red hula hoop. Mussburger thinks it's a terrible idea that will cost the company millions of dollars, so he encourages Barnes to go forward with production. "Congratulations, kid, you've really outdone yourself. Reinvented the wheel," Mussburger says.

At first Barnes's hula hoop is a massive flop, and Mussburger is elated. But after a few months, one young boy finds a hoop rolling down a sidewalk and begins to hula with it as a nearby school lets out. A massive crowd of children sees him playing with the hula hoop, and they are mesmerized. They run, screaming toward the nearest toy store to buy their own. The hula hoop is a huge hit, and Barnes becomes a media darling all over again, even getting a congratulatory phone call from President Dwight Eisenhower. Mussburger is furious and begins plotting to get rid of Barnes.

Barnes's downfall begins when he starts to believe his own reviews. Success goes to his head, and he becomes a lazy, self-important executive who treats his employees like mere commodities—cogs in a machine who can be replaced at will. When Buzz the elevator operator tries to show Barnes a design he's come up with for a bendy straw, Barnes fires the poor fellow. Buzz falls to the ground weeping, begging for his job back, and Barnes barks, "Get up! We don't crawl at Hudsucker Industries!" He's come full circle. But what goes around comes around. Mussburger fires him after discovering Amy Archer's true identity. "That dame, she got your throat pretty well slit," Mussburger says before throwing Barnes out of the executive suite. "When you're dead, you stay dead. You don't believe me, ask Waring Hudsucker! Tough luck, kid. You had a short climb up. It's a long way down."

By New Year's Eve, Barnes is out of a job, out of luck, and out of hope. He winds up inexplicably drunk in a beatnik juice bar, where Archer finds him and desperately tries to apologize for causing his downfall. He won't have any of it and returns to the Hudsucker building, where he climbs onto the ledge, has second thoughts, and turns to go back inside—but Aloysius, the deathlike maintenance man who replaces the nameplates of each fired executive, has closed and locked the windows. Barnes slips and falls, plummeting toward the sidewalk, just as Waring Hudsucker had a month earlier. However, a second or two before he should hit the ground, time stops, and Barnes hovers—suspended in midair. The camera jumps to Moses, who takes care of the clock tower atop Hudsucker Industries (and just so happens to be the voice of the narrator). He has stuck his broom handle into the clockworks. "Strictly speaking, I'm never supposed to do this," Moses says to the camera. "But have you got a better idea?"

Moses' intervention is a classic example of *deus ex machina*—God out of a machine—a literary device used to resolve hopeless situations in unforeseen and, some would say, wholly unbelievable ways. Cleverly, Moses is God *in* the literal machine, and the allusion to the God-as-clockmaker analogy is deliberate. The teleological idea that creation is so detailed and finely tuned that an intelligent designer must have made it is one that has been used in attempts to "prove" God's existence for centuries. In the seventeenth century, some Western philosophers theorized that the clock (that is, creation) was so well calibrated that the maker (that is, God) need not intervene further. The scene where Moses stops time using his broom handle seems to suggest that God does, in fact, still intervene in history—at least from time to time.

Deus ex machina derives its name from Greek tragedy, where a crane—the *machina*—would be used to lower actors playing deities down from above the stage. What happens next takes this device to its literal extreme. Waring Hudsucker—dressed in white, encircled by an electric halo, and singing "She'll Be Comin' Around the Mountain When She Comes"—is slowly lowered into the frame next to where Barnes is suspended in midair. Hudsucker asks Barnes why he never delivered the blue letter to Mussburger, which reveals, among other things, that Hudsucker killed himself because of a broken heart. He was in love with the woman Mussburger married, and, despite all of his material success, he had never gotten over the loss of the one thing he really cared about in life.

Hudsucker's letter also unveils his final wishes—an ersatz will—that says when the board finds someone to replace him as president of the company, all of his stock shares are automatically transferred to his successor. "Despair looks only to the past, in business and in love. The future is now. The future is now. When our future president needs it, Waring Hudsucker hereby bequeaths him his second chance," the letter concludes. "Deliver that letter in the morning," a laughing Hudsucker says before ascending out of the scene.

Meanwhile, Moses and Aloysius, who has entered the clockworks to see why time has stopped, are engaged in an epic struggle between good and evil. At one point, Moses socks Aloysius, knocking out his dentures, which go scuttling across the metal scaffold on which they are fighting. Moses defeats Aloysius, finally knocking him over the scaffold and into the huge gears of the clock, which has begun ticking again. Outside, Barnes resumes his plummet toward the ground, only to be jerked to a halt a few feet above the sidewalk. Moses has used Aloysius's dentures to jam the gears of the clock, literally stealing life out of the jaws of death.

In the end, Barnes gets his girl, reuniting with Amy as she cries into her carrot juice at her favorite beatnik juice bar (where Steve Buscemi makes a cameo appearance as the hipster bartender). Moses resumes his role as the film's narrator, telling us in a voice-over that Barnes returned to his role as president of Hudsucker Industries, where he goes on to rule with "wisdom and compassion" for many years. Mussburger, distraught by the divinely inspired turn of events, crawls out on the ledge of his office and threatens to jump. Instead, he ends up committed to the "booby hatch," where he had plotted to send Barnes. The circle is complete.

The film ends with a smiling Barnes in the Hudsucker boardroom introducing his latest invention, a red Frisbee, which he tosses whimsically out the open, 44th-floor window.

THE MORAL OF THE STORY ...

One of my all-time favorite on-screen depictions of God comes in Kevin Smith's 1999 film *Dogma*. The role of the Almighty is played by two actors—Bud Cort (Harold of *Harold and Maude*) and the Canadian singer-songwriter Alanis Morissette. Cort's God is a geriatric gentleman who comes to earth to indulge his divine pastime—skee ball—but never speaks. Morissette's God is a whimsical, if all-powerful, female incarnation of the Creator who turns up at the end of the film when the humans—and a couple of fallen angels—have made a mess of things. The two avenging angels have slaughtered hundreds of people, and the corpses litter the streets, surrounded by other scenes of material destruction.

Morissette's God doesn't speak either, but for good reason. We're told by the Metatron (God's transcriptionist played by Alan Rickman) that if human beings were to hear God's voice in all its awesomeness, their heads would literally explode. Clearly troubled by the devastation she sees, Morissette's God surveys the damage carefully, rubs her hands together, and—poof—all is made right. The dead are living and the streets are restored to order. She does this not because humanity deserves to be rescued by her divine intervention, but simply because she loves her children and her creation. Morissette's God restores order entirely as an act of grace—thoroughly unmerited and unearnable.

Much the same way, in *The Hudsucker Proxy*, the unseen hand of God grants Barnes an underserved second chance. Turning the time-space continuum upside down, God stops time and, through grace, allows Barnes to live and make things right.

Through the medium of a screwball comedy, the Coens present a loving, if subtle, portrait of a God who reaches into the world to save us from ourselves, even—or perhaps especially—when we least deserve it.

FARGO

CHAPTER 6

FARGO

"I'm carrying quite a load here."

THE FOREST

A killing spree rips through the suburban bliss of Brainerd, Minnesota. Heavily pregnant police chief Marge Gunderson is charged with cleaning up the mess and solving the crime—the result of a botched kidnapping scheme set in motion by the greed of a spineless local car salesman, Jerry Lundegaard. With a combination of savvy detective work, unfailing good cheer, and old-fashioned Midwestern politeness, Gunderson uncovers the plot and tracks down the killers-for-hire—the weaselly Carl Showalter (who meets his gruesome end in a wood chipper) and his near-catatonic partner Gaear Grimsrud.

THE TREES

"This is a true story."

So begins *Fargo*, the Coen brothers' Northern Gothic masterpiece, perhaps the finest example of a Judeo-Christian morality play in all of American cinema. Here the long roads and tall trees of the rural South are replaced by the ethereal, snowy world of the Coens' native Minnesota, where good and evil are as clearly delineated as night and day. While there are no explicit religious references in the film, it stands apart from the rest of their oeuvre as the clearest depiction of a moral universe plagued by wickedness.

A black screen precedes the first photography of the film—a wide shot of a two-lane highway in a whiteout blizzard. The vast whiteness is punctured at first only by the silhouette of a bird and then by the headlights of an American-model sedan towing another behind it. The printed prologue that starts the film claims the story we're about to see is based on true events that took place in Minnesota in 1987. In their inimitably oblique way, the brothers later said their film was not based on actual events, yet neither claim changes the essential truth of the story.

The film's protagonist, Marge Gunderson (Frances McDormand), the preternaturally cheery chief of police in Brainerd, Minnesota, is seven months pregnant with her first child when news of a triple homicide rouses her from bed in the middle of the night. The chaos is set in motion by a morally weak car salesman, Jerry Lundegaard (William H. Macy) who has hired two soulless criminals, Carl Showalter (Steve Buscemi) and Gaear Grimsrud (Peter Stormare), to kidnap his wife, Jean (Kristin Rudrüd)—the daughter of the wealthy, surly businessman Wade Gustafson (Harve Presnell)—so he can collect the ransom and rescue himself from financial ruin. Rather than turn to his wife or father-in-law for help, Lundegaard, felled by the fatal flaw of pride, instead turns to a cockamamy scheme that ends in profound tragedy for all those he claims to love.

While the film's main characters surely are not purely symbolic, an allegorical interpretation based on their actions hovers over the plot.

The villains — Lundegaard, Showalter, Grimsrud, and Gustafson — manifest the seven deadly sins. Showalter is captive to lust, as demonstrated by his penchant for prostitutes. Grimsrud, who shares Showalter's indulgence in prostitutes, is ruled by gluttony; he seems incapable of sating his craving for pancakes. He is also something of a sloth, unable to muster the energy even to engage in polite conversation with Showalter as they make the four-hour drive from Brainerd to Minneapolis. At their hideout by Moose Lake, Grimsrud is content to sit catatonic in front of a black-and-white television set that gets only one channel. All four men are hot-tempered and liable to bouts of wrath — homicidally so in the case of Showalter and Grimsrud, who kill six people without conscience. Lundegaard envies the lifestyle his father-in-law enjoys, overextends himself financially, and engages in malfeasance to the tune of $320,000 — falsifying loan records at GMAC for vehicles that don't exist. He's even willing to jeopardize his wife in order to maintain his upper-middle-class status. Both he and Gustafson are blinded by pride, as is Showalter, who meets his demise when he refuses to share with Grimsrud the relatively paltry worth of an Oldsmobile Sierra — part of the original ransom deal with Lundegaard.

Conversely, Marge Gunderson represents all that is good and righteous, the poster child for the four cardinal virtues of justice, fortitude, prudence, and temperance. She embodies the laws of both humanity and God — not as a judgmental voice but as the rule of love, compassionately upholding order and respect for all of God's children. Saint Augustine defined the four cardinal virtues — deriving their name from the Latin *cardo*, meaning "to hinge," since the entire moral universe hinges on them — this way: "Temperance is love giving itself entirely to that which is loved; fortitude is love readily bearing all things for the sake of the loved object; justice is love serving only the loved object and therefore ruling rightly; prudence is love distinguishing with sagacity between what hinders it and what helps it."[9]

Marge is a Christ figure, a mouthpiece for God, willingly risking (with unfailing good cheer) her own safety in order to vanquish evil and restore moral order. In the face of death, she is, quite literally, a fecund life-giver, poised to deliver a child—and a new beginning —into the world. She also could be viewed as the Madonna, the gentle, willing vessel of the Lord. Perhaps her initials, M. G., even indicate this interpretation as Mother of God.

The Rev. Bob Barron, my friend and a Catholic priest, suspects the film's title, *Fargo*, describes Marge's mission in life—to go far out to the margins in order to bring wayward sinners back to grace. "She represents Christ; she represents the church at its best," Barron says. "She's able to go out to the margins but she's not compromised by it. She's not drawn into that world. She's able to go into it in a very intense way; she's not afraid of it . . . yet she's not attracted to it, she's not drawn into its power. And that's what the church at its best ought to do."[10]

Another way of understanding Marge's role is to view her through the lens of H. Richard Niebuhr's theological models for how faith functions in the world. Marge is "Christ transforming culture," an agent for change who is in the world but not of it. It's the last of five paradigms that Niebuhr described in 1959 to explain the tension between Christianity and culture. Niebuhr's other four paradigms are:

- *Christ against culture* describes efforts to isolate Christianity from culture and its evils to keep it holy.

- *Christ of culture* says, basically, that Jesus was part of culture when he walked the earth, so Christianity should actively engage culture.
- *Christ above culture* says that culture can't be all bad because it's an extension of God's creation, but that it is Christianity's duty to foster good values in culture, with an eye toward the eternal.
- *Christ and culture in paradox* finds balance in the friction between Christ and culture.

Niebuhr's "Christ transforming culture" (also known as the "conversionist" point of view)—supposes that Christianity has the power (and the responsibility) to convert culture to a more godly orientation and that it's possible to make the world a better place in this lifetime and not just in the hereafter.

Fargo, a dark comedy featuring moments of hilarity juxtaposed against scenes of brutal violence, follows in the tradition of American Catholic author Flannery O'Connor, whose short stories and novels similarly use comedy and violence to depict the sometimes shocking way that grace can break into a fallen world during moments of tragedy and confusion. Throughout the film, violent scenes are bookended by images from Marge's humble, righteous life.

With her husband Norm (John Carroll Lynch), Marge lives in a modest home in the central Minnesota working-class city of Brainerd. Historically, Brainerd has depended largely on the railroad and paper mills for its economy. It is the home of the mythical folk hero Paul Bunyan; a large, animated statue of Bunyan wielding an axe stands on the edge of town and figures prominently in *Fargo* (although the statue and the Blue Ox Bar pictured in the film are not the actual landmarks).

Norm, a soft-spoken lug of a gentleman, paints ducks and duck decoys as a hobby—or perhaps as a living. When we first meet him, he has just entered an oil painting of a mallard duck in a contest to appear on a United States postal stamp. Each time we see Norm and Marge at home, they are in bed—sleeping, watching television, or cuddling at the end of a long day. Their home is a haven, as is their uncomplicated love and loyalty. It's interesting that Norm's contest entry is a mallard, a duck that mates for life. When we see the Gundersons at the local smorgasbord for lunch, they walk side by side carrying trays loaded with chicken fricassee and Swedish meatballs to their table, both waddling—Marge because she is heavy with child and Norm because he's just heavy—like a couple of ducks. Their relationship is a moral anchor, the embodiment of fidelity and normalcy.

On the surface, the Lundegaard home could appear to be a similar haven, but we quickly learn that whatever stability and fidelity seem to be present are as superficial as the veneer that covers most of their furniture. There is no indication that Jean Lundegaard is anything but a loving, faithful homemaker, nor is there any indication that she aspires to anything beyond her middle-class comfort. She may be from wealthy stock, but she displays none of the pretensions of her birth family. Her home has none of the trappings of wealth, unlike her father's office, which is decorated with expensive oil paintings and bronze cowboy sculptures. Whatever aspirations Jerry, Jean's husband, has to a swankier lifestyle appear to be entirely self-motivated.

While the film says nothing explicit about their spiritual leanings, the audience might picture them as a God-fearing, churchgoing Lutheran family. One might imagine the Lundegaards to be pillars of the community—Jerry respected as a good husband and loving father. But it's no more than a facade. When Jerry learns that Jean has been violently kidnapped by Showalter and Grimsrud, his concern for their teenage son, Scotty (Tony Denman), is an afterthought. When he does check in on Scotty, who is tearfully sitting on his bed between his hockey stick and his accordion, it is clear Lundegaard is more concerned with keeping the kidnapping a secret than he is about his son's mental state, telling the boy that if any of Jean's friends call the house, he should say, "Mom is in Florida with Pearl and Marty." The scene in Scotty's room is the last time we see the boy, and we're left to speculate about his fate when the kidnapping goes wrong, his mother and grandfather wind up dead, and his father is in shackles on his way to prison.

For his part, Jerry's father-in-law, Wade Gustafson—whose only emotions are anger and pride—is even more transparently unfeeling about his family. While he tells Lundegaard that "Jean and Scotty never have to worry" about their financial security, when faced with a ransom demand of $1 million, Gustafson's first instinct is to bargain the amount down to $500,000. Throughout his interactions with Lundegaard and the kidnappers, his chief concern is not his daughter's safety but his money. Surely Scotty will inherit his grandfather's immense wealth, but he is left a veritable orphan, deprived of his mother's love and his father's presence. In this story, the wages of sin is death, and the sins of the fathers are visited upon the son in a tragic, visceral way.

Conversely, we know that Marge will naturally impart goodness to her child from the way she interacts with those around her. While she is a shrewd policewoman—quick and decisive when examining a crime scene in pursuit of the truth—she never lords her wisdom over anyone else. Sitting in the squad car after her initial examination of the triple homicide committed by Grimsrud—the point-blank execution of a state trooper who stops their car and the merciless shooting of a young couple who happened upon the scene—Officer Lou (Bruce Bohne) tells her that he's got an all-points bulletin out for a car with plates that begin with the letters DLR. "I'm not sure I agree with you a hunnert percent on your police work there, Lou," she says, gently. "I think that vehicle there probably had dealer plates—DLR?" Lou is momentarily cowed, but she immediately diffuses any tension by telling him a silly joke: "Say, Lou, ya hear the one about the guy who couldn't afford personalized plates, so he went and changed his name to J2L 4685?" "Yah, that's a good one," Lou says, comforted.

When Marge interviews the two blonde hookers (Larissa Kokerhort and Melissa Peterman) who had sex with Showalter and Grimsrud the night before the murders and kidnapping, she is respectful and affirming, unfazed by their descriptions of the sexual encounter with the two criminals. The women are real bubbleheads, but Marge never lets on that she thinks them fools, instead going out of her way to acknowledge how helpful they've been. The only time Marge's good nature is tested is during her second interview with Jerry Lundegaard at the car dealership. In response to his rudeness, Marge's ever-present smile disappears momentarily. "Sir, you have no call to get snippy with me," she says. "I'm just doin' my job here."

Perhaps actress Frances McDormand's personal story helped her deliver such a nuanced, tender performance (for which she won the Oscar for Best Actress) as Marge Gunderson. McDormand's father is a retired Disciples of Christ minister who specialized in helping struggling congregations regroup. Her sister, also a Disciples of

Christ minister, spent time as a prison chaplain. McDormand must have firsthand knowledge of the challenges and rewards of serving the least among us with compassion and grace.

McDormand's character Marge is conscientious and thorough. In one scene, the local barman reports an unsettling encounter with a customer (Showalter) who was looking for a prostitute because he was "goin' crazy down there at the lake" and bragging about having killed the last man who crossed him (Gustafson, who Showalter guns down on the roof of a parking lot during a botched ransom delivery). On her way home Marge dutifully takes a ride by Moose Lake just in case. She spots the Oldsmobile Sierra parked at a lake house and calls it in, but she doesn't hesitate for a second before scrambling out of the car, gun drawn, to investigate.

There, in the most gruesome scene in the film, she comes face-to-face with Grimsrud, who is feeding Showalter's body into a wood chipper, splattering the pristine white snow with blood and bone fragments. Just moments earlier, Grimsrud killed Jean because she wouldn't stop screaming. Then he took an axe to Showalter—who buried the ransom money in the snow by the side of a highway rather than share it with his accomplice—because he refused to split the car with him. When Marge approaches Grimsrud and trains her gun on him, she can't be heard over the roar of the wood chipper. She could shoot him right there, but instead she gives him the chance to surrender—even going so far as pointing to the police star on her hat so he'll know she's a cop. Grimsrud flees across the lake and Marge pursues him, waiting to get a clean shot of his leg rather than shooting him in the back.

With Grimsrud in the back of her squad car, Marge delivers a simple yet profound soliloquy about right and wrong: "So that was

Mrs. Lundegaard in there. I guess that was your accomplice in the wood chipper. And those three people in Brainerd. And for what? For a little bit of money. There's more to life than money, you know. Don't you know that? And here ya are, and it's a beautiful day. Well, I just don't unnerstand it."

In a Wittgensteinian way, Marge, who is unfailingly good, cannot comprehend such unrestrained evil. That is not to say that she does not understand it in a literal sense, but that she lacks the capacity to sympathize with it. It is so far beyond the realm of possibility in her rightly ordered moral universe that it is simply and totally unfathomable. In Marge's world, there's right and there's wrong, and never the twain shall meet.

The film ends on the night of Grimsrud's arrest, with Marge climbing back into bed with Norm, who has just learned his mallard was chosen for the three-cent stamp. He's feeling dejected because his painting won't be gracing the twenty-nine-cent stamp instead. "It's just the three-cent. Hautman's blue-winged teal got the twenty-nine cent. People don't much use the three-cent," he mutters. "Oh, for Pete's sake, of course they do!" Marge assures him. "Every time they raise the darned postage, people need the little stamps.... That's terrific. I'm so proud of you, Norm. Heck, Norm, you know, we're doin' pretty good."

Patting her pregnant belly and whispering, "Two more months," Norm tells Margie he loves her. "I love you, too, Norm."

And that is a true story, if ever there was one.

THE MORAL OF THE STORY . . .

I have a bumper sticker on my car that reads "Love wins." A pastor-friend gave it to me. His church produces them by the crateful. Whenever I'm stuck in traffic, invariably a fellow motorist will honk and give me the thumbs-up or shout out the window that they like what it says. It's a simple platitude, but it's powerfully true. In a world marred by random violence and discord, we need to be reminded that in the end love, not hate, is victorious.

Sometimes it feels like love is a whisper lost in a hurricane. But like light in the darkness, love is exponentially more powerful than hate, and life is more powerful than death.

Marge Gunderson embodies that notion. By being a literal and figurative life-bearer in the face of violence, chaos, and death, she was able to hold the moral center. Her example of kindness, respect, and compassion is truer than any horror story, fictional or otherwise. May we all choose love and pierce the darkness with its eternal light.

CHAPTER 7

THE BIG LEBOWSKI

"The Dude abides."

THE FOREST

Sometimes there is a man for his time and place. An unlikely hero charged with setting the moral order straight. In early 1990s Los Angeles, that man is Jeffrey "The Dude" Lebowski, a seemingly hapless burnout who spends his time smoking weed and bowling with his friends Walter Sobchak—a personal security specialist and Vietnam veteran who sees conspiracies at every turn—and the sweet-tempered simpleton Donny Kerabatsos.

In a case of mistaken identity, The Dude becomes embroiled in the fake kidnapping of Bunny, trophy wife of the other Jeffrey Lebowski, a wheelchair-using millionaire philanthropist whose wealth isn't exactly what it seems. Thugs sent by pornographer Jackie Treehorn, to whom Bunny Lebowski owes money, come to collect at The Dude's apartment, rough him up, and pee on his rug. In his quest to be compensated for his ruined rug, The Dude, with Walter and Donny by his side, must battle a band of hapless nihilists posing as the kidnappers before the truth of Bunny's disappearance (and a host of other lies) are revealed for what they are.

THE TREES

In Genesis, the opening book of the Hebrew Scriptures, the author tells the story of Sodom and Gomorrah, two cities destroyed by God's wrath for their unrepentant lasciviousness. Before hellfire and brimstone rain down on the twin towns, Abraham, God's chosen dude, argues with the Almighty not to destroy them. God, in turn, agrees not to lay them waste as long as Abraham can prove there are fifty righteous souls living there. When Abe has a hard time coming up with fifty, he bargains with God to accept forty-five innocents, then thirty, then twenty, and finally a measly ten. When God's avenging angels can find only one righteous man—Abraham's nephew Lot—in two cities, God cues the sulfur rain, and the cities go up in flames, though Lot is spared.

The account of Sodom and Gomorrah gave rise to the lore of the *lamed-vavniks*. According to various kabbalistic teachings, at any given time in history there are thirty-six righteous people (*lamed-vavniks* take their name from the Hebrew letters *lamed*—meaning "thirty"—and *vav*—"six") on whom the fate of the world rests. If even one of them were to perish, God would destroy the world. The *lamed-vavniks*—also known as *menschen* in Yiddish—don't know the identity of one another and in fact don't even know that they themselves are counted among the righteous thirty-six. Sometimes the *lamed-vavniks* appear to be humble fools—slackers or burnouts, in the parlance of our time—but the rest of us should take heed. We never know when we might meet one of the thirty-six, so we should treat everyone as if the fate of the world rests on their unassuming shoulders.

If ever there was a *lamed-vavnik* in the annals of celluloid history, it's Jeffrey "The Dude" Lebowski. As *The Big Lebowski* opens, a tumbleweed floats through the streets of Los Angeles. Down from the Hollywood Hills, it rolls past Benito's burrito stand to the shores of the Pacific Ocean, dreamlike, and we hear the voice of The Stranger (Sam Elliot), deep and drawling like the Marlboro Man—or perhaps the Metatron (according to rabbinic tradition, the angel who is God's celestial scribe)—beginning to tell a tale for the ages:

A way out west there was this fella, fella I want to tell you about, fella by the name of Jeff Lebowski. At least that was the handle his lovin' parents gave him, but he never had much use for it himself. This Lebowski, he called himself The Dude. Now, Dude, that's a name no one would self-apply where I come from. But, then there was a lot about The Dude that didn't make a whole lot of sense to me. And a lot about where he lived, likewise. But then again, maybe that's why I found the place so durned innarestin' . . .

Now this story I'm about to unfold took place back in the early nineties—just about the time of our conflict with Sad'm and the Eye-rackies. I only mention it 'cause sometimes there's a man—I won't say a hee-ro, 'cause what's a hee-ro?—but sometimes there's a man.

And I'm talkin' about The Dude here—sometimes there's a man who, well, he's the man for his time 'n place, he fits right in there—and that's The Dude, in Los Angeles. And even if he's a lazy man, and The Dude was certainly that—quite possibly the laziest in Los Angeles County, which would place him high in the runnin' for laziest worldwide—but sometimes there's a man, sometimes there's a man.

The Dude (Jeff Bridges) is a simple, unsuspecting fellow; that much is certain. The aging hippy antihero. A mellow, pot-smoking, bowling burnout who lives alone in a modest apartment in the Venice neighborhood of Los Angeles—the modern-day Sodom and Gomorrah where individualism, instant gratification, materialism, objectification, and unchecked aggression rule the day. The Dude—or Duder, His Dudeness or El Duderino, if you're not into that whole brevity thing—is a walking anachronism and a kindly soul. He is an ideologue, a passionate pacifist who loves his friends, judges not, and mostly minds his own business. "Live and let live" is his philosophy. But he has a firm moral center. He knows what's right and what's wrong and isn't afraid to stand up for the cause of love and peace.

Trouble finds The Dude often, though he rarely goes looking for it. When he returns from Ralph's supermarket with his half & half in one hand and bowling ball in the other, two goons jump him in his apartment, shove his head in the toilet, and pee on his Oriental rug. It's a case of mistaken identity. They've appeared to collect on the debt of a woman named Bunny Lebowski, the young trophy wife of the *other* Jeffrey Lebowski—a wealthy, wheelchair-using philanthropist who lives in a mansion in Pasadena. Bunny, we learn, owes money to the infamous pornographer Jackie Treehorn (Ben Gazzara). Flummoxed by the whole violent encounter and mourning the defilement of his beloved carpet, The Dude turns to his two closest confidants and bowling teammates, Walter Sobchak (John Goodman) and Theodore Donald "Donny" Kerabatsos (Steve Buscemi), for consolation, if not guidance.

Walter, a hulking man who proudly wears his dog tags from his Vietnam War days, is bombastic, quick-tempered, and dogmatic. Donny, on the other hand, is a complete innocent, a childlike, wan wisp of a man for whom Walter has great affection, if no patience.

"Shut up, Donny! You're out of your element!" is a frequent refrain any time Donny dares to speak his mind or ask a question. Walter and Donny are like a Laurel and Hardy of the loser set, and The Dude is the captain-cum-guru who pilots their little ship of fools.

Walter is all about retribution and suggests that The Dude track down the other Jeffrey Lebowski to make things right. "I'm talking about drawing a line in the sand, Dude. Across this line you do not ..." he shouts, and then interrupts himself to correct The Dude, who had called the offending pee-er "this Chinaman." "Also, Dude, *Chinaman* is not the preferred, uh ... Asian-American. Please," Walter says.

The next day we learn a little bit more about The Dude's background as he pays a visit to the other Lebowski's mansion and gets a tour of the trophy room, courtesy of Lebowski's patsy assistant, Brandt (Philip Seymour Hoffman). When Brandt erroneously concludes The Dude never went to college, The Dude gently corrects him, saying, "Well, yeah, I did, but I spent most of my time occupying various, um, administration buildings, smoking Thai stick, breaking into the ROTC, and bowling. I'll tell you the truth, Brandt, I don't remember most of it."

The Dude's countercultural air doesn't sit well with the *other* Jeffrey Lebowski (David Huddleston) when the two finally meet. The Big Lebowski, as The Dude comes to think of him, immediately dismisses him as a lowlife looking for a handout and tells him as much. Their exchange goes something like this:

Lebowski: "Hello! Do you speak English? *Parla usted Inglese*? I'll say it again. Did I urinate on your rug?"

The Dude: "Well, no, like I said, Woo peed on the rug."

Lebowski: "Hello! Hello! So every time — I just want to

understand this, sir — every time a rug is micturated upon in this fair city, I have to compensate the —"

The Dude: "Come on, man, I'm not trying to scam anybody here. I'm just —"

Lebowski: "You're just looking for a handout like every other — are you employed, Mr. Lebowski?...

"Are you employed, sir?"

The Dude: "Employed?"

Lebowski: "You don't go out looking for a job dressed like that in the middle of a weekday."

The Dude: "Is this a — what day is this?"

Lebowski: "But I do work, so if you don't mind —"

The Dude: "No, look. I do mind. The Dude minds. This will not stand, ya know, this will not stand, man. I mean, if your wife owes —"

Lebowski: "My wife is not the issue here! I hope that my wife will someday learn to live on her allowance, which is ample, but if she doesn't, sir, that will be her problem, not mine. Just as your rug is your problem, just as every bum's lot in life is his own responsibility regardless of whom he chooses to blame. I didn't blame anyone for the loss of my legs, some Chinaman in Korea took them from me, but I went out and achieved anyway. I can't solve your problems, sir. Only you can."

The Dude: "Ah, f–it."

Lebowski: "Sure! F–it! That's your answer. Tattoo it on your forehead. That's your answer for everything. Your revolution is over, Mr. Lebowski. Condolences! The bums lost! My advice to you is to do what your parents did! Get a job, sir! The bums will always lose — do you hear me? The bums will always lose!"

On his way out of the Lebowski mansion, The Dude tells Brandt that the old man invited him to take any rug in the house; and as another of Lebowski's servants hauls out a large Oriental rug behind him, The Dude meets Bunny Lebowski (Tara Reid) by the pool, where she is painting her toenails emerald green. She's young, vapid, and overtly sexual—the quintessential gold digger—and she offers to perform a sexual favor on The Dude for $1,000. When The Dude mistakes the beach-blonde fellow passed out on a raft with a bottle of Jack Daniels for her boyfriend and asks whether he'll mind, Bunny answers: "Uli doesn't care about anything. He's a nihilist."

The rug caper sets in motion a chain of events that unfurls in classic Coen brothers form, with a kidnapping (or so everyone believes), mistaken identities, more violence, double-crosses, and a cast of strange characters, including Maude Lebowski (Julianne Moore)—the Big Lebowski's avant-garde artist daughter who decides to sire a child with the unwitting Dude. There's also a hostile, pederast rival bowler named Jesus (John Turturro), and The Stranger who appears at the bowling alley bar dressed in cowboy attire, complete with a white ten-gallon hat, and orders a Sioux City Sarsaparilla. "I like your style, Dude," he says. "Just one thing, Dude: D'ya have to use s'many cuss words?" ("The f—are you talking about?" is The Dude's reply.)

Through every twist and turn of the wacky plot, which includes several bowling-themed dream sequences, The Dude always tries to do the right—or righteous—thing. He's unfailingly kind. When his dorky landlord Marty (Jack Kehler) appears at the door of his apartment to ask him to come to his one-man dance performance and give him notes, The Dude happily agrees. When Walter pulls a gun on Smokey (Jimmie Dale Gilmore), a mild-mannered rival bowler who accidentally slips his toes over the line while bowling a strike, The Dude chastises his friend and explains that Smoky is a pacifist, a conscientious objector during the Vietnam War, who has psychological problems. ("He's fragile, man!") And when Donny dies of a heart attack during an encounter with a band of would-be nihilists, The Dude accompanies Walter to a promontory to scatter his ashes, which they've carried from the mortuary in a coffee can. As Walter delivers his eulogy, laced with nonsensical references to the Vietnam War, which Donny didn't fight in, and manages to scatter the ashes all over The Dude, The Dude gets momentarily angry — "Everything's a f–ing travesty with you, Walter!" — but ends up giving the big lug a hug.

On the path to the plot's conclusion, The Dude is pummeled time and again, like a martyr for the cause of righteousness. He's beaten by Jackie Treehorn's thugs on at least two occasions, verbally assaulted by the Big Lebowski, attacked by marmot-wielding nihilists in the comfort of his own bathtub, menaced by a deranged Corvette owner with a crowbar, involved in three car accidents, clobbered by Maude's boy-toy musclemen, doped into a stupor with a drug-laced White Russian (mixed for him by the pornographer Jackie Treehorn), hit in the head with the Malibu police chief's coffee cup — "You f–ing fascist!" he screams — and thrown out of a taxi-cab for protesting the driver's musical selection: the dreaded Eagles' "Peaceful Easy Feeling." Watching The Dude endure these physical hardships calls to mind a Hebrew proverb that says, "Though the righteous [the *menschen*] fall seven times, they rise again."[11]

As the film hurtles to its conclusion, in short order The Dude discovers that Lebowski has concocted Bunny's alleged kidnapping in order to steal money (in the form of a "ransom") from the Lebowski

Little Urban Achievers foundation, which, Maude tells The Dude, is comprised entirely of funds from her late mother's estate. Lebowski doesn't have any real wealth of his own but lives off of his wife's inheritance.

Bunny, it turns out, hadn't really disappeared at all, nor was she kidnapped. She simply went to visit friends in Palm Springs and forgot to tell her husband. The suitcase Lebowski gave The Dude that was allegedly filled with the $1 million ransom was actually empty. Lebowski thought that way he'd be able to keep the $1 million for himself.

The Dude and Walter confront Lebowski at his mansion in a hilarious scene in which at one point Walter, convinced that Lebowski was faking his disability, drags him from his wheelchair and tries to make him stand. Unfortunately, the only thing Lebowski seems to be telling the truth about is his paralysis.

The Dude: "You thought Bunny'd been kidnapped and you could use it as a pretext to make some money disappear. All you needed was a sap to pin it on, and you'd just met me. You thought, hey, a deadbeat, a loser, someone the square community won't give a shit about."

Lebowski: "Well? Aren't you?"

The Dude: "Well, yeah."

If The Dude's life philosophy—his Dudeology, if you will—could be summed up in one phrase, it would be, "Just take it easy, man." It's a worldview that is profound in its simplicity, and one that is so appealing to rabid fans of *The Big Lebowski* that an actual religion has grown up around it. A few years back, one clever fan, Oliver Benjamin, a freelance journalist/graphic designer and self-proclaimed "unprofessional musician" who lives in Thailand, created the website *www.dudeism.com*—the online home of the official Church of the Latter-Day Dude. (The church ordains Dudeist priests online and for free—for real!—and I myself am a duly ordained Dudeist priest capable of lawfully presiding at weddings in most states.)

Benjamin describes Dudeism this way: "The idea is this: Life is short and complicated, and nobody knows what to do about it. So don't do anything about it. Just take it easy, man. Stop worrying so much whether you'll make it into the finals. Kick back with some friends and some oat soda and whether you roll strikes or gutters, do your best to be true to yourself and others."[12]

Benjamin argues that the closest spiritual cousin to Dudeism is Zen Buddhism, the philosophy that emphasizes experience over theory or the study of religious texts. Zen, adherents say, is the finger pointing at the moon, rather than moon itself or the pathway to it. "Like Zen, Dudeism isn't into the whole doctrinal thing; we prefer direct experience of takin' 'er easy, and often contemplate two indiscernible Coens to achieve that modest task," the "Arch Dudeship" Dwayne Eutsey writes in the church's "Take It Easy Manifesto."[13]

Walter Sobchak serves as the theological opposite of The Dude. An ardent legalist who is tethered to his past—as opposed to the here and now of the Dude-iverse—Walter encourages acrimony and confrontation and sees conspiracies at every turn. He is also a proud Jew, a converted Polish Catholic who made the leap to Judaism when he married Cynthia, his ex-wife of five years. He goes ballistic when his team is scheduled to bowl on Saturday, or Shabbat, the Jewish day of rest. "I don't roll on Shabbas!" he howls, and accuses the scheduler, who has a German surname, of being an anti-Semite.

When Walter complains that The Dude has made him break the Sabbath by driving him to the Big Lebowski's mansion on the night The Dude realizes he's been double-crossed, The Dude accuses him of not really being Jewish. Walter responds angrily, "What do you think happens when you get divorced? You turn in your library card? Get a new driver's license? Stop being Jewish? I'm as Jewish as f–ing Tevye!" The Dude says he's living in the past, to which Walter replies, indignant and screaming as usual, "Three thousand years of beautiful tradition from Moses to Sandy Koufax—you're g–dd–n right I live in the past!"

Whether The Dude is a Zen icon is debatable—"Yeah, well, that's just, ya know, like, your opinion, man," he might say. But *The Big Lebowski* is surely the Coen brothers' most blatantly spiritual (and eminently quotable) film. However you choose to describe The Dude's philosophy or theology, it is most surely not dogmatic, legalistic, Fascistic, or narrow.

In the final scene of the film, after all of the double-crosses have been uncovered, the nihilists vanquished, and errant wives returned to their marital beds (at least theoretically), The Dude encounters The Stranger one last time. The Dude, who is rolling with Walter in the semifinals of their bowling league tournament, wanders up to the bar to order a couple of oat sodas (beers) and finds The Stranger sitting there.

"Hey man, how are ya? I wondered if I'd see you again," The Dude says. The Stranger, smiling, asks him how he's been. "Ah, you know, strikes and gutters, ups and downs" is his Zenlike answer. As The Dude leaves The Stranger to his Sarsaparilla, The Stranger says, "Take it easy, Dude. I know you will," to which The Dude responds in his final words of the film, "Well, you know, The Dude abides."

The Stranger recognizes the profundity of this statement and says, in a spiritually soaked soliloquy that ends the film:

I don't know about you, but I take comfort in that. It's good knowin' he's out there, The Dude, takin' her easy for all us sinners. Shoosh. I sure hope he makes the finals. Welp, that about does her, wraps her all up. Things seem to've worked out pretty good for The Dude 'n Walter, and it was a purt good story, dontcha think? Made me laugh to beat the band. Parts, anyway. Course, I didn't like seein' Donny go. But then, I happen to know that there's a little Lebowski on the way. I guess that's the way the whole durned human comedy keeps perpetuatin' itself, down through the generations, westward the wagons, across the sands a time until — aw, look at me, I'm ramblin' again. Well, I hope you folks enjoyed yourselves.

Takin' her easy for all us sinners. That's what a *lamed-vavnik* does. That is what grace is, the kind of grace Jesus (the Son of God, not the pedophilic bowler) talks about in the Gospels. The kind of grace that The Dude, in his inimitable way, exudes in every one of his relationships. An unexpected kindness, granting unmerited goodwill, giving someone a break when they don't deserve it, showing up for the semis even when you have a bad attitude just because it means so much to the rest of the team, hugging it out instead of slugging it out. *Abide.* It means "to wait patiently for something." Or "to endure without yielding, to accept without objection," according to the official word-defining dudes at Merriam-Webster. Abiding is no easy feat, especially in a culture that is success driven, instant-gratification oriented, and pathologically impatient like ours. True abiding is a spiritual gift, mastered only, it would seem, by the more fully evolved among us.

The Dude abides. Amen and hallelujah.

THE MORAL OF THE STORY...

Be kind.

Treat others as you want to be treated yourself.

You never know when the stranger you meet on the road may be an angel in disguise.

Whatever you have done for the least of these, you've done for me.

The Big Lebowski is, at its heart, about the Golden Rule. Whether The Dude is a *lamed-vavnik*, an angel in disguise, or merely a kind-hearted loser, we should treat him as he treats us—with respect and compassion. No one knows who is or isn't a *lamed-vavnik*, not even the *menschen* themselves. Therefore, we should all live as if we, and all those we encounter, are *lamed-vavniks*, righteous souls with whom the eventual healing of the world abides.

CHAPTER 8

O BROTHER, WHERE ART THOU?

"Everybody's lookin' for answers."

THE FOREST

Ulysses Everett McGill, a fast-talking, smart-aleck convict serving time for practicing law without a license, escapes a chain gang in rural 1930s Mississippi while shackled to a couple of dim-witted prisoners, Pete Hogwallop and Delmar O'Donnell. In this modern retelling of Homer's epic *The Odyssey*, Everett's quest is to reunite with his wife, Penny, and their gaggle of young daughters. But in order to accomplish that, he convinces Pete and Delmar that he's leading them to a $1.2 million booty he stole and buried at his family homestead.

Along their journey, the three convicts are pursued by a demonic police chief, befriend a young black blues guitarist who has recently sold his soul to the devil, run afoul of the Ku Klux Klan, and are befriended by the opportunistic governor, Pappy O'Daniel (who's running for reelection against a Klansman), and become surprise musical stars as the old-timey gospel group The Soggy Bottom Boys.

Still, it's only an act of God (in the form of a man-made flood) that saves Everett and his cronies from their execution and allows Everett and Penny finally to reunite.

THE TREES

Like one of King David's millennia-old laments, the song of alienation and suffering sung by Ulysses Everett McGill and the Soggy Bottom Boys, "Man of Constant Sorrow," eventually becomes the anthem of his salvation. "For in this world I'm bound to ramble," he sings. "But there is one promise that is given: I'll meet you on God's golden shore."

Throughout *O Brother, Where Art Thou?* Everett (George Clooney) contends that he has no use for faith, for the superstitious religious beliefs he might well say are the acme of foolishness. But like the voice of the Holy running through human history, the film's soundtrack of old-timey gospel songs reaffirm the faith that our antihero — an escaped convict desperate to reconcile with his estranged family — constantly ridicules.

The film begins with an invocation from the filmmakers in the opening words of Homer's *Odyssey*:

> *O Muse!*
> *Sing in me and through me tell the story*
> *Of that man skilled in all ways of contending*
> *A wanderer, harried for years on end …*

Despite Joel Coen cheekily insisting in numerous interviews that the brothers have never read Homer's epic poem about the wanderer Odysseus (or Ulysses in Roman lore), the quote seems to be an invitation to the audience to view the story they're about to see as more than what meets the eye. It is, perhaps, an allegory, the big story of humankind told through the trials and tribulations of one little man, Ulysses Everett McGill. Like *The Odyssey*, *O Brother* begins *in medias res*, in the middle of things, with Everett and the two dim-witted cohorts to whom he is chained, Pete Hogwallop (John Turturro) and Delmar O'Donnell (Tim Blake Nelson), on the run from a chain gang. The trio manages to make their getaway by hitching a ride with a blind black man trundling slowly down the tracks on a hand-cranked railroad car. Here again, in the words of the blind prophet, we understand that this is more than just a slapstick crime caper. Rather, it is a spiritual odyssey. The blind oracle, who calls the escaped convicts "my sons," prophesies about the future of their endeavor, saying:

> You seek a great fortune, you three who are now in chains. And you will find a fortune, though it will not be the fortune you seek. But first, first you must travel a long and difficult road, a road fraught with peril, mm-hmm. You shall see things wonderful to tell. You shall see a — a cow on the roof of a cotton house, ha! And, oh, so many startlements. I cannot tell you how long this road shall be, but fear not the obstacles in your path, for fate has vouchsafed your reward. Though the road may wind, yea, your hearts grow weary, still shall ye follow them, even unto your salvation.

Set in rural 1930s Mississippi, in the throes of the Great Depression, *O Brother* tells the comically desperate tale of Everett, Pete, and Delmar, who, in addition to being on the run, are on a mission to reclaim a $1.2 million treasure Everett says he has stolen and buried at the family homestead. The entire *mise en scene* of the film is a dusty, faded ocher, a deliberate choice on the part of the filmmakers, who had the film digitally color-corrected in post-production to give the otherwise verdant Mississippi landscape a soft, sepia hue.

The trio's first stop on their road to freedom is at the broken-down farm of Pete's cousin, Washington Hogwallop (Frank Collison), who raised horses in better days and has the smithy tools to knock off the fugitives' shackles. Washington's wife has abandoned him and his rifle-wielding young son — "Mrs. Hogwallop up and R-U-N-N-O-F-T." After a supper of nearly spoiled horse stew, the three bed down in the barn, only to be awakened by a police lynch mob, who set fire to the barn to flush the convicts out. Washington has double-crossed them, turning in his own cousin for the reward money. "They got this Depression on, and I gotta do for me and mine," he tells an incensed Pete, who then threatens to murder him. The scene evokes one of the persistent themes of the film — that of exactly who and what family is.

In one of many narrow escapes, Everett, Pete, and Delmar flee to the woods, where their midday lunch of roast gopher is interrupted by a singing church congregation, clad in white, heading down to the river for a mass baptism. Seeing his chance for redemption — spiritual and otherwise — Delmar, the archetypal holy fool of whom the Coens are so fond, clambers into the river, where the pastor dunks him fully clothed beneath the water, just as John the Baptist did for Jesus in the River Jordan. "Well I'll be a son of a bitch, Delmar's been saved," Everett exclaims.

Delmar emerges from the river proclaiming that he has been re-deemed. "The preacher said all my sins is washed away, including that Piggly Wiggly I knocked over in Yazoo," Delmar shouts. When Everett reminds him that he'd previously claimed to be innocent of that particular crime, Delmar continues, unfazed. "Well I was lyin', and the preacher said that that sin's been washed away too. Neither God nor man's got nothin' on me now!" At that, Pete decides to get baptized too.

In their recently procured getaway car, the theological conversation continues, with Everett scoffing at his companions' simple faith. "Even if it did put ya square with the Lord, the state of Mississippi is more hard-nosed," he says. "You shoulda joined us, Everett, it couldn't a hurt none," Delmar replies. "Join you fools in superstition? Thank you anyway," Everett sniffs.

Yet as if to demonstrate that Delmar's simple faith is true and his redemption genuine, the sweet-souled con asks Everett to pull over to pick up a young black man standing at a crossroads with a guitar. It's a radical move, considering the social and racial mores of the time and place. We learn that the gentle young man is Tommy Johnson (real-life blues artist Chris Thomas King) who had gone to the crossroads at midnight to sell his soul to the devil in exchange for guitar virtuosity. "Oh, son, for that you traded your everlastin' soul?" Delmar says sympathetically. "Well, I wasn't usin' it," Tommy says.

Everett finds this all terribly amusing, laughing as he says, "Ain't it a small world, spiritually speakin'? Pete and Delmar just been baptized and saved. I guess I'm the only one here who remains unaffiliated." When Pete asks what the devil looks like, Everett, ever the loquacious know-it-all, responds with a stereotypical portrait of "the Great Satan hisself": red and scaly with a bifurcated tail and a pitchfork. Tommy corrects him, saying the devil he met the night before was white with hollow eyes, and he travels with a mean hound dog. The description matches that of the leader of the police posse hot on the escapees' trail.

Tommy leads the trio to a radio station in Tishomingo, Mississippi where he's heard that a man will pay $10 a pop to "sing into a can." At the WEZY studio, they meet the blind station manager (Stephen Root), who agrees to record them as the fictitious Soggy Bottom Boys, singing the old-timey spiritual, "Man of Constant Sorrow." It's a providential turn of events that, unbeknownst to them, will lead to the trio's eventual freedom—and perhaps even their salvation—when it becomes a runaway hit on the radio all over the state.

On their way out of the radio station, the group runs into Menelaus "Pappy" O'Daniel (Charles Durning), the governor of Mississippi, who is in the midst of a hotly contested reelection campaign. O'Daniel, a gruff, rotund biscuit flour mogul, owns the radio station. His opponent in the gubernatorial race is a squirrelly fellow named Homer Stokes (Wayne Duvall), who we later learn is corrupt in more ways than one.

In the middle portion of the film, Everett, Delmar, and Pete meet a series of larger-than-life characters straight out of Homer's *Odyssey*. First is George "Baby Face" Nelson (Michael Badalucco), a notorious, bipolar bank robber more interested in the fame—or infamy—he garners as a gangster than in any of his ill-gotten gains. (Interestingly, in 1933 the real-life Nelson notoriously robbed the First National Bank in Brainerd, Minnesota, the setting for the Coens' film *Fargo*.) Nelson's moodiness is reminiscent of Homer's shape shifter Proteus, a Greek god who was able to tell the future but would change his form to avoid having to do so. Proteus would only divulge his knowledge of the future to those who could capture and imprison him.

Next Everett, Delmar, and Pete are lured to a stream by the song of three beautiful washerwomen—Homer's Muses—who get them drunk and turn Pete into a frog, or so Delmar presumes. Everett and Delmar and Pete the frog (carried in a shoe box) next meet Big Dan Teague (John Goodman), a traveling Bible salesman with an eye patch, a clear reference to the one-eyed monster Polyphemus the Cyclops bested by Odysseus. Contrary to *The Odyssey*, where Odysseus escapes after blinding Polyphemus by stabbing him in the eye while the monster is passed-out drunk, Teague beats Everett and Delmar to a pulp, steals their money, and squishes Pete the frog.

Goodman's character is also a clear commentary on faux Christianity. "What do I sell? The truth, every blessed word of it, from Genesis down to Revelations," he says. "Yes, the word of God, which, let me say, there's damn good money in during these days of woe and want. People want answers, and Big Dan sells the only book that's got 'em." Obviously, Big Dan — the so-called Christian — doesn't buy what he's selling.

When Everett and Delmar finally reach Everett's hometown, we meet Penny Wharvey McGill (Holly Hunter), Everett's ex-wife, who, like Odysseus's wife, Penelope, is being courted by a suitor in her husband's absence. Penny's beau is Vernon T. Waldrip (Ray McKinnon), to whom she plans to be married the next day. Everett confronts Penny, who has told their six young daughters that their dad was hit by a train (rather than telling them he's doing time for practicing law without a license). "They look to me for answers," she says, justifying her decision.

Vernon, a real drip who is running Homer Stokes's campaign for governor, is "bona fide," Penny says. With that, she spurns Everett, who desperately wants to reconcile with his wife and children. Meanwhile, Pete (who is still a man and not a dead frog) has been captured by the sadistic police chief — Satan hisself — and is about to be hung, when he gives up the location of the goods where Everett and Delmar are headed. This disloyalty haunts him. It's the one sin he can't forgive himself for, full-immersion baptism or not.

The trio is reunited in a movie theater, when Pete turns up, accompanied by a phalanx of other prisoners. He warns Everett and Delmar not to go after the treasure because the police know where they're headed. That night, Everett and Delmar break Pete out of jail, only to stumble onto a huge Ku Klux Klan rally.

The Klan gathering has all the trappings of a religious event, with the white-hooded Klansmen, who call each other "brothers," processing in formation, singing a spiritual that goes, in part, "I'm death, I come to take the soul, leave the body and leave it cold.... O death, won't you spare me over till another year." The Klan's grand wizard, cloaked in scarlet red, announces that they're going to lynch a black man, Tommy. "Sweet Jesus, we gotta save 'im!" Pete shouts, running toward the lynch mob without a second thought for his own safety—and Everett and Delmar fast on his heels.

The trio disrupts the gathering, and we discover that Big Dan is one of the ringleaders and Homer Stokes is the grand wizard. Big Dan meets his end when the trio cuts the cables supporting a huge flaming cross, and it falls on the one-eyed monster. The three escapees and Tommy make their way to the town hall where Penny is having dinner at a Stokes fund-raiser. Wearing long bushy beards as their disguise, the three men take to the stage and end up performing their Soggy Bottom Boys song, "Man of Constant Sorrow." The crowd goes wild until Stokes interrupts, announcing that the men are convicts, race mixers who disrupted a lynch mob "in the performance of its duties." But the audience isn't buying into Stokes's race baiting and boos him until he is run out of the building on a rail — literally.

Ever the opportunist, Pappy O'Daniel seizes his chance to win over the voting public and takes to the stage, doing a jig that's intended to say that not only is he a fan of the Soggy Bottom Boys; he believes they've been truly redeemed. "Looks like Homer Stokes is the kind of fella who wants to cast the first stone," he tells the crowd. "Well, I'm with you, folks. I'm a forgive-and-forget Christian, and I say if their rambunctiousness and misdemeanoring is behind them — it is, ain't it, boys? — well then, I say, by the power vested in me, these boys is hereby pardoned!"

The governor even proclaims that the Soggy Bottom Boys will be part of his "brain trust" in the next administration. Penny agrees to forgo her wedding to Waldrip and remarry Everett, but she'll only do it if he can find her original wedding ring, which is in the rolltop desk at the "ancestral manse" — a cabin in a valley that's about to be flooded by the state to make way for a hydroelectric power plant.

Everett, Delmar, Pete, and Tommy, thinking their woes are behind them, head out to the McGill cabin, only to find Satan and his posse waiting. Three black men — Homer's Fates, perhaps — are digging their graves, singing a mournful Negro spiritual: "Got to go to that lonesome valley ... nobody else can go there for you, no." Four nooses are hung from a tree, and the boys are sentenced to death, despite their protestations of a full pardon. "It went out on the radio," Delmar pleads. "We ain't got a radio," the devil says. Satan doesn't have the ears to hear words of mercy.

At last it would appear that Everett has come to the end of the road, the finale of his long odyssey to find reconciliation and the answers to his questions. He can't talk his way out of this tight spot.

He can't rationalize his way to salvation or make any bargain with the devil. Everett has but a single recourse left: an appeal to God's grace. He begins to pray, though not in the fast-talking parlance he is so used to invoking. His is as genuine and desperate a prayer as ever has been prayed. Cowering on his knees with the noose literally hanging around his neck, Everett says,

> O Lord, please look down and recognize us poor sinners. Please, Lord. I just want to see my daughters again. I've been separated from my family for so long. I know I've been guilty of pride and sharp dealing. I'm sorry I turned my back on you, forgive me. We're helpless, Lord. For the sake of my family, for Tommy's sake. For Delmar's and Pete's. Let me see my daughters again, Lord. Help us, please.

God's answer comes in a resounding rush, as floodwaters deluge the valley and set Everett and the other captives free, saving them from the jaws of death and, we presume, drowning their persecutors and the devil himself. The former convicts are redeemed from the wages of their sin and emerge from the floodwaters clinging to a wooden casket. Tommy pops out of the waters riding the rolltop desk that supposedly contains Penny's wedding ring. Delmar proclaims it a miracle, but Everett, having yet another change of heart (or at least of mind) calls him ignorant. "Well, it never fails. Again you hayseeds are showin' you want for intellect. There's a perfectly scientific explanation," Everett says, to which Pete counters, "That ain't the tune you was singin' back at the gallows!"

Still, Everett tries to explain the divine intervention away.

> Any human being'll cast about in a moment of stress. No, they're flooding this valley so they can hydroelectric up the whole darn

state. Yes, sir, the South is gonna change. Everything's gonna run on a paying basis. Out with the spiritual mumbo-jumbo and backward ways. We're gonna see a brave new world where they hook us all up to a grid. Yes, a veritable age of reason. Like the one they had in France. Not a moment too soon.

It is precisely then that Everett notices the cow standing on the roof of a cotton house.

The film draws to a close with Everett and Penny reunited, their young daughters singing the Stanley Brothers' gospel tune, "Angel Band," while the blind prophet slowly moves farther on down the railroad tracks into the distance.

> *My latest sun is sinking fast, my race is nearly run*
> *My strongest trials now are past, my triumph has begun*
> *O come Angel band, come and around me stand*
> *O bear me away on your snow-white wings to my immortal home.*

THE MORAL OF THE STORY …

O Brother, Where Art Thou? leaves us with an answer to its eponymous question. Our brother is each person we see, for we are all the children of God — of equal worth, no matter our race or status in society — and bona fide, one and all, only by the flooding power of God's audacious saving grace.

Though never explicit, the film presents a nuanced picture of the Christian idea of grace — that God extends unmerited goodwill to all of creation, including those humans who don't even recognize God's very existence. Intellect can get in the way of seeing God clearly, as is the case with Everett, who protests having any real faith except for when he's most desperate (and his true heart is revealed). It's the simpleton, Delmar, who accepts God's grace freely and without reservation, believing his sins are washed away once and for all time when he's baptized. It's Delmar's simple faith that saves him through grace — nothing he does or doesn't do himself. While he refuses to recognize it (yet), the same is ultimately true for Everett. God saves him in spite of himself. And that, in a nutshell, is grace.

THE MAN WHO WASN'T THERE

CHAPTER 9

THE MAN
WHO WASN'T THERE

"Sometimes the more you look,
the less you really know."

THE FOREST

Ed Crane is the second-chair barber in a two-barber shop. He's stuck in a passionless marriage to his employer's sister, Doris, but doesn't have the will to change anything about his life until a traveling businessman tells him about an investment opportunity: dry cleaning.

Doris is having an affair with her boss, Big Dave Brewster, who runs the local department store (owned by Big Dave's wife's family). Ed discovers the affair and decides to blackmail Big Dave in order to raise the money to invest in the dry-cleaning venture. Big Dave murders the traveling businessman, mistaking him for the real blackmailer, and Ed kills Big Dave, but lets Doris (an alcoholic given to blackouts) take the blame. On the day Doris's murder trial is scheduled to begin, she commits suicide. When the traveling businessman's body eventually is discovered at the bottom of a quarry, Ed is charged with his murder, convicted, and sentenced to death.

THE TREES

In a black-and-white world, Ed Crane (Billy Bob Thornton) lives in the grays. His hair is as gray as the incessant cigarette smoke that encircles his head. His clothes are gray, and so are his dark eyes. Set in 1949 Santa Rosa, California, *The Man Who Wasn't There* is an epic noir tale of postmodern existential angst, with Crane as its listless narrator and protagonist. Ed's life has happened by default. Foot problems (fallen arches) kept him out of the military service in World War II. He became a barber by accident, not design, marrying into his wife's family business. Even his sexless marriage was more happenstance than conscious choice. Ed and Doris (Frances McDormand) met on a blind date, he tells us dispassionately. "She said she liked it I didn't talk much. A couple weeks later she suggested we get married."

When we meet Ed, he suspects that Doris is having an affair with her boss, "Big Dave" Brewster, proprietor of Nirdlinger's Department Store, which is owned by Big Dave's wife's family. Even his cuckolding doesn't seem to elicit any passionate response from Ed, who moves through his life like a specter. "The signs were all there, plain enough," he says of Doris's affair with Big Dave. "Not that I was gonna prance about it, mind you. It's a free country."

Ed is clearly dissatisfied with his lot in life but is too hobbled by emotional and spiritual inertia to do anything about it until a traveling salesman arrives at Guzzi's—the barbershop where Ed works second-chair to his brother-in-law Frank—one afternoon for a haircut, even though he wears a toupee. His name is Creighton Tolliver (Jon Polito), and he's come to Santa Rosa to get Big Dave to invest $10,000 in a dry-cleaning venture. Big Dave blows him off, and Ed sees an opportunity to escape his soulless routine at the barbershop and, perhaps, the life he shares with Doris. It's his chance to become a man that people notice and not just a mere ghost or "the barber."

Later that evening, Ed visits Tolliver at his hotel. At first, Tolliver has no idea who he is. "I didn't recognize you without your smock," he says. Ed tells him he wants to be his silent partner and that he can come up with the $10,000 in a week. Tolliver makes a pass at him, and even that doesn't cause Ed's near catatonia to crack. "You're outta line," is the only thing he says.

To raise the money, Ed decides to blackmail Big Dave, sending him an anonymous letter that says the letter writer knows about the affair and will tell Ed Crane about it if Big Dave doesn't come up with $10,000. During a pre-Christmas bash at Nirdlinger's, Big Dave summons Ed to his office, where he confides in him about the blackmail and asks him what he should do, though he never lets on that Doris is the married woman with whom he's having an affair. Ed tells him to pay the blackmailer and be done with it. Big Dave complies, but eventually he traces the money to Tolliver and uncovers Ed's double-cross.

When Ed and Doris return from the wedding one of her Italian relatives whom she scorns, Doris is passed out in an alcoholic stupor. Big Dave calls Ed, summoning him to the empty Nirdlinger's store. Asking, "What kind of man are you?" Big Dave confronts Ed about the blackmail. The two come to blows, and as Big Dave tries to strangle his blackmailer, Ed stabs him fatally in the neck with a knife-shaped cigar trimmer. (Big Dave claimed he took the knife off a Japanese soldier during the war, but we later discover that Big Dave was assigned to desk duty in San Diego during the war and never saw combat, despite his bragging about being a war hero.)

The next day, two detectives show up at Guzzi's barbershop to inform Ed that they've arrested Doris for Big Dave's murder. Ed is characteristically stoic—though he does consult with a friend, Walter Abundas (Richard Jenkins), about who to hire as a defense lawyer. Walter says Freddy Riedenschneider (Tony Shalhoub) of Sacramento is the best there is, so Ed hires him. Doris's brother, Frank (Michael Badalucco), mortgages the barbershop to pay Doris's legal fees. Freddy is an arrogant, bombastic bore who meets with Ed in the restaurant of a Santa Rosa hotel to outline how much his legal services are going to cost—including all his meals. (He's ordered almost everything on the menu and is staying in one of the hotel's luxury suites.) Ed's only reaction is to blink mutely.

That night, Ed is home alone, smoking as always, when the door-bell rings. It's Ann Nirdlinger Brewster (Katherine Borowitz), Big Dave's strange widow. She has huge eyes and doesn't seem to blink. On her head is a bizarre veiled hat resembling a flying saucer that, perhaps, is a deliberate style choice—given that she tells Ed an un-believable story about Big Dave being abducted by aliens while they were on vacation a few years before. "He never touched me again," she says, adding that she knows Doris didn't kill Big Dave because the government had orchestrated his death in order to cover up any evidence of alien life. Ann is delusional and clearly more comfortable believing her husband stopped having sex with her because he was traumatized by aliens than admitting that he was having an affair. UFOs make a number of appearances in the film, including a dream sequence within the story. Ed in particular has the sense of being deeply alienated from the world around him.

When Freddy meets with Doris and Ed at the prison for the first time, talking nonstop as he tries to figure out what his defense strategy will be, Ed confesses to killing Big Dave and reveals to Doris that he knew about the affair. Freddy dismisses this tack as a viable defense strategy, saying it's not enough to have the husband back up the wife's story. No one will believe it, he says, even if it's the truth. The only person who could corroborate Ed's story is Tolliver, but he has disappeared with Ed's $10,000.

At their second meeting, the slick defense attorney has come up with a defense strategy based in part on a theory from quantum physics:

> They got this guy in Germany. Fritz something or other. Or is it? Maybe it's Werner. Anyway, he's got this theory. You wanna test something, you know, scientifically — how the planets go 'round the sun, what sunspots are made of, why the water comes out of the tap — well, you gotta look at it. But sometimes you look at it, your looking changes it. Ya can't know the reality of what happened, or what would've happened, if you hadn't stuck in your own g–dd–n schnozz. So there is no "what happened." … Looking at something changes it. They call it the "uncertainty principle." Sure, it sounds screwy, but even Einstein says the guy's on to something. Science. Perception. Reality. Doubt. Reasonable doubt. I'm sayin' that sometimes the more you look, the less you really know.

It's a thoroughly postmodern idea of reality and truth — if there is even such a thing as truth. The world was in a state of flux in the years following World War II. Society was changing. Morals and mores were up for grabs, and the more science learned about the universe, the less it seemed to know. The universe was random. Nothing was certain.

The idea that nothing is certain, that we can't trust our own perception of what is real, true, or meaningful, plays into the kind of existential angst that consumes Ed. He makes his living as a barber but doesn't consider himself to be a barber. He's a narrator who doesn't like to talk. He's a husband who hasn't "performed the sex act," as he puts it, with his wife for years. He's a murderer whose wife is on trial for the crime he committed. As much "sense," if you can call it that, as Freddy's reasoning might have made in 1949, it had even more resonance in 2001 (when the film was released) in the wake of a former president—a philanderer himself—who argued publicly about what the definition of *is* is.

On the day the trial is set to begin, the judge announces that there will be no trial because Doris has committed suicide. (We later learn that she was in the early stages of pregnancy when she died and that Big Dave was likely the father, as she and Ed had not had sex in many years.) Freddy collects his papers, his fee, and his bags and returns to Sacramento, grumbling about what a waste it was for Doris to kill herself because he had such a brilliant defense planned for her.

Financially ruined and mourning his sister's death, Frank sinks into a deep depression, begins drinking heavily, and stops coming into the barbershop. Ed becomes the first-chair barber and hires an assistant, only to be terribly disappointed when the young barber turns out to be more of a motormouth than Frank had been. Walking home after closing up shop one evening, Ed again describes his feelings of utter alienation from the world around him. "When I walked home, it seemed like everyone avoided looking at me, as if I'd caught some disease," he says. "This thing with Doris, nobody wanted to talk about it. It was like I was a ghost walking down the street. And when I got home now, the place felt empty. I sat in the house, but there was nobody there. I was a ghost. I didn't see anyone. No one saw me. I was the barber."

Ed has become infatuated with his friend Walter's daughter, Birdy (Scarlett Johansson), a pretty teenage pianist. In the classical music she plays, Ed finds comfort and peace. He offers to manage what he believes is Birdy's burgeoning musical career, paying for private lessons and even taking her to see a famous piano teacher in Sacramento in the hopes that he'll take Birdy on as his student. The piano teacher, Jacques Carcanogues (Adam Alexi-Malle), a smug effete, is unimpressed with Birdy's playing and sends Ed packing.

In the car on the way home, Birdy makes an overt sexual advance toward Ed, who is still unable to act, even on his most basic desires. His only response is to shout, "Heavens to Betsy!" and drive off the road. He awakens in the hospital, with two detectives hovering over him. They tell him he is being charged with murder. "Big Dave?" Ed mutters, thinking his crime has finally caught up with him. But it's not Big Dave's murder he's charged with — it's Tolliver, whose badly beaten body was found in his car submerged in a reservoir. (We learn that Big Dave killed him.)

Ed once again hires Freddy as a defense attorney, and the lawyer again concocts a defense based on Werner Heisenberg's uncertainty principle. The trial is proceeding well, with Freddy telling the jury to "not look at the facts but at the meaning of the facts." And then he says, "The facts have no meaning." The jury seems to buy the convoluted reasoning, and even Ed says he is beginning to believe it. But then Frank, obviously out of his mind from weeks of nonstop drinking and grief over his sister's death — for which he blames Ed — interrupts the proceedings, screaming, "What kind of man are you!" Freddy asks for a mistrial and gets it, but Ed can't afford to hire him a third time.

Ed winds up with a local attorney, who throws him on the mercy of the court, hoping to avoid the death penalty. The strategy fails, and Ed is sentenced to death in the electric chair. On death row, Ed writes his memoirs for a tabloid crime magazine. We realize then that the story he's narrated is the tale he's being paid five cents a word to write for the magazine. Is it all true? Some of it? None of it? What is true, anyway?

The film ends with Ed strapped into the electric chair, leaving us with the final monologue: "I guess I'm sorry about the pain I caused other people, but I don't regret anything. Not a thing. I used to. I used to regret being the barber. I don't know where I'm being taken. I don't know what I'll find beyond the earth and sky. But I'm not afraid to go. Maybe the things I don't understand will be clearer there, like when a fog blows away. Maybe Doris will be there. And maybe there I can tell her all those things they don't have words for here."

THE MORAL OF THE STORY . . .

Live your life. Don't just be spectators.

Make a leap of faith.

Doubts—about what is right, what is true, real, better, or best—can paralyze us. But that's not what we were put on this earth by our Creator to be. We should embrace life's rich pageant, and, as the German poet Goethe said, "Plunge boldly into the thick of life."

Ed was paralyzed by the choices he wasn't able to make. That paralysis led to the calcification of his heart. Afraid to make a decision, take a chance, or reach out for the love he deserved, Ed passed through life like a sleepwalker.

We only get one chance to live, and it passes all too quickly if we don't seize it. On our deathbeds, none of us wants to be filled with regret for the things we've done or, more painfully perhaps, the things we've left undone.

INTOLERABLE CRUELTY

CHAPTER 10

INTOLERABLE CRUELTY

"Love is good."

THE FOREST

Miles Massey is arguably the most successful divorce attorney in Los Angeles. Author of the ironclad "Massey prenup," Massey is able to win divorce cases even for the most egregious philanderers without giving his conscience a second glance. Massey meets his match in the beautiful but scheming gold digger Marilyn Rexroth, whose husband—the millionaire industrialist Rex Rexroth—has hired Massey to represent him in his divorce from Marilyn.

When in open court Massey exposes Marilyn for the conniver that she is, she turns her vengeful attention to Massey, who is besotted with her. In a series of double- and triple-crosses, Marilyn dupes Massey into marrying her—and then leaves him penniless and homeless. In the end, however, true (if blind) love wins, Massey gives up the divorce racket, and lives happily ever after with Marilyn.

THE TREES

It is tempting to sum up the moral value of *Intolerable Cruelty* with one word: intolerable. There are so few redeeming or likable qualities about the characters in this double-crossing con-man farce that to tease any spiritual lessons from their machinations seems, on the surface, a fool's errand.

The pure Hollywood story here is told largely from the perspective of Miles Massey (George Clooney), a seemingly conscienceless and successful (perhaps because of his missing moral center) divorce attorney in Beverly Hills. When we first meet him, he has been secured as counsel for the philandering wife of a daytime TV producer named Donovan Donaly (Geoffrey Rush); she has been caught in flagrante delicto with the pool boy (despite the glaring absence of a pool).

When Donaly catches her and pulls a handgun on the illicit pair, the wife (Stacey Travis) stabs him in the arse with his own Daytime Television Lifetime Achievement Award. Donaly, in a move even Massey praises as showing "remarkable foresight," takes Polaroid pictures of his fresh wounds. Undaunted, Massey lays out his defense plan for the wife, which involves boldly fabricated claims of chronic physical abuse and a homosexual affair. What is clear is that Massey is ruthless, conniving, and extremely good at what he does. He wins a handsome settlement for the wife, leaving Donaly destitute and living on the streets.

Massey's lack of regard for the sanctity of marriage is painfully obvious, even before he delivers a monologue about matrimony's shortcomings. "The problem is, everyone is willing to compromise. That's the problem with the institution of marriage. It's based on compromise. Even through its dissolution," Massey says. "The entire process will find an equilibrium point based on the skill of the individual lawyers. Then both parties will go home with their portion of the staple factory."

When his colleague retorts that compromise is what life is all about, Massey is indignant. "That's not life. That's death. Struggle and challenge and ultimate destruction of your opponent—that's life," he says. And that's dark. Not exactly the stuff of which your typical frothy comedy is made.

Massey meets his match—professionally and morally—in his next divorce case, where he has been hired to represent the husband, Rex Rexroth (Edward Herrmann), a wealthy industrialist caught on tape cheating with a blonde bimbo—his downfall brought about by his wife's private detective, Gus Petch (Cedric the Entertainer), whose professional catchphrase is "I'm gonna nail your ass!"

Rexroth's estranged wife is the smolderingly charming Marilyn (Catherine Zeta-Jones). Far from being devastated by her husband's infidelity, we learn that catching him in the act is part of her master plan to marry well and divorce better, leaving her an independently wealthy and unattached woman. Massey is immediately captivated by Marilyn, drawn to her twisted morality as much as her unmistakable physical beauty.

With the help of his feckless legal assistant, Wrigley (Paul Adelstein) —and in the first instance of what will become an elaborate plot of double- and triple-crosses—Massey manages to expose Marilyn's calculated con in court (with the aid of Marilyn's own private eye, Petch), leaving her with nothing in the divorce settlement. She, in turn, plots revenge not on her ex-husband but his divorce attorney, Massey. She shows up at his office with a new fiancé in tow, a goofy

Texas oil baron named Howard D. Doyle (Billy Bob Thornton), and asks Massey to draw up a prenuptial agreement—the fabled, impenetrable "Massey prenup." Later, at their wedding reception, Howard eats the prenup with a side of barbeque sauce, proclaiming to his new, not-so-blushing bride, "I love you! I trust you!"—at which point Massey thinks he's got Marilyn's scam figured out.

However, there's another double-cross. Still besotted with the newly divorced Marilyn when he runs into her at a divorce lawyers convention in Las Vegas six months later, Massey pursues her like a man obsessed. Over a would-be dinner she appears to let her guard down at last. Talking about Marilyn's best friend, Sarah Battista-O'Flanagan-Sorkin (Julia Duffy), an oft-divorced maven who lives alone in a 46-room estate, with only her peptic ulcer to keep her company, Massey says, "There's a certain point when you've achieved your goals . . ." and Marilyn finishes his thought: "you realize that you're still not satisfied."

They've both lost their appetites and return to their rooms. Soon Massey's phone rings and it's Marilyn on the other line, despondent, she says, because Sarah Sorkin has just died. "And she was alone!" Marilyn weeps. Massey rushes to her side; they kiss and soon are standing before a justice of the peace at the Wee Kirk O' the Heather wedding chapel. Because, he presumes, Marilyn is insanely wealthy from her divorce settlement with Howard the oil baron, Massey insists she sign the Massey prenup to protect her assets. She grudgingly agrees, and they are wed.

Back in the honeymoon suite, before they consummate the marriage, Marilyn tears up the prenup, saying that she trusts Massey and doesn't need a piece of paper to protect her. The next day, the normally meticulously dapper Massey is disheveled when he turns up to deliver his keynote address, tentatively titled "Nailing Your Spouse's Assets," at the annual congress of the National Organization of Matrimonial Attorneys Nationwide (NOMAN, with its slogan "Let NOMAN Put Asunder"). Instead of reading his prepared statement, Massey rips it in two (just as Marilyn had done to her Massey prenup), instead waxing poetic about true love:

> I stand before you naked, vulnerable, and in love. *Love*. It's a word we matrimonial lawyers avoid. Funny, isn't it? We're frightened of this emotion, which is, in a sense, the seed of our livelihood. Well, today Miles Massey is here to tell you that love need cause us no fear. Love need cause us no shame. Love is good. Love is good.
>
> I am, of course, aware that these remarks will be received here with cynicism. Cynicism — that cloak that advertises our indifference and hides all human feeling. Well, I'm here to tell you that that cynicism which we think protects us in fact destroys. Destroys love, destroys our clients, and, ultimately, destroys ourselves.
>
> Colleagues, when our clients come to us confused and angry and hurting because their flame of love is guttering and threatens to die, do we seek to extinguish that flame so that we can sift through the smoldering wreckage for our paltry reward, or do we fan this precious flame, this most precious flame, back into loving, roaring life? Do we counsel fear or trust? Do we seek to destroy or build? Do we meet our clients' problems with cynicism or with love?
>
> The choice is, of course, each of ours. For my part, I've made the leap of love, and there's no going back. Ladies and gentlemen, this is the last time I will address you as the president of NOMAN — or as a member. I intend to devote myself to pro

bono work in East Los Angeles or one of those other—God bless you all.

It's a real *Jerry McGuire* moment, complete with the stunned silence followed by one man's slow-clapping that builds into a cheering, standing ovation from the entire crowd. Love seems to have conquered all, until Wrigley, enjoying a celebratory Scotch with Massey while watching TV in the hotel bar, spots Howard the oil baron—or rather the actor who was playing Howard—acting as a doctor in a soap opera and quickly realizes that Marilyn has double-crossed Massey. Again. She wasn't a millionaire divorcée when she married Massey in the Wee Kirk and then tore up the prenup. She wasn't a woman in love. She was the cold, calculating con artist that Massey always thought her to be.

Marilyn begins divorce proceedings against Massey immediately, laying claim to his palatial estate while he crashes on Wrigley's couch. He's chastised by the law firm's senior partner, a cadaverous yellow-eyed geezer named Herb Myerson (Tom Aldredge), who embodies all that Massey fears becoming. "This woman has shamed, humbled, and disgraced the entire firm," Myerson wheezes. "Tell you something, smart guy. You thought you had it. Trust. Marriage. All your g—dd—n love, love, love! Now, you listen to me. I'm gonna talk to you about the g—dd—n law. We serve the law! We honor the law! And sometimes, Counselor, we obey the law. But, Counselor, this is not one of those times."

So Massey does the logical thing: he hires a hit man—Wheezy Joe (Irwin Keyes)—to kill Marilyn. But in yet another twist, before Wheezy Joe can do the deed, Massey learns that Rex Rexroth has died of a massive coronary (in flagrante once again) and that he never changed his will. Marilyn stands to inherit the Rexroth fortune. She's rich! They're still married, and without the Massey prenup that she tore up, Massey would get half of the Rexroth estate in any divorce.

In a bumbling caperesque scene, Massey and Wrigley try to head off Wheezy Joe before he whacks Marilyn, but she's too wily for them and has already paid off the hit man to kill Massey. The two divorce lawyers struggle with Wheezy Joe and spray him in the face with Mace, and the would-be assassin mistakes his pistol for his asthma inhaler, shooting himself in the mouth.

The film ends as it began, with Massey and Marilyn facing each other across the table of a divorce lawyer's office. They proclaim their love for one another, despite (or perhaps because of) having double-crossed each other numerous times. Perhaps they love each other precisely because of their matching twisted morality. Maybe what they have is a true and pure love, based on knowing each other's faults and accepting them. Massey, now the wealthier party—the one his ironclad prenup is designed to protect—signs a new copy of the agreement and then promptly tears it up, proving that their marital bond is one based on trust and, yes, love.

THE MORAL OF THE STORY ...

While the vehicle is surely flawed—in his review of *Intolerable Cruelty* the venerable Roger Ebert gave it 2 ½ stars, calling it, generously, an "imperfect screenplay"—the message is simple and clear: marriage is sacred; and love, even a deeply imperfect love, is good. Even if it doesn't conquer all.

Our love may be imperfect too, but it's still the best thing we have and can do in this world. Jesus' command to his disciples—and to all of us who would like to call ourselves his followers—was to love. Without boundaries. Without judging others as unworthy. Without discriminating. We are commanded to love, selflessly and wholeheartedly, as God loves us. We might not always get there, but if we err in the direction of love, we'll find ourselves on the path to salvation, and, ultimately, perfection.

THE LADYKILLERS

CHAPTER 11

THE LADYKILLERS

"Behold, there is a stranger in our midst come to destroy us."

THE FOREST

A widow, Ms. Marva Munson, the quintessential Southern church lady, lives in a quiet Mississippi town where her biggest concern has to do with a neighbor boy who plays hip-hop music too loud for her liking. One morning, she answers the door to find the charming, if eccentric, Professor Goldthwait H. Dorr on her doorstep, looking to rent the spare bedroom in her house. Dorr, a goofy dandy who resembles the poet Edgar Allan Poe (with whom he is obsessed) tells Ms. Munson that he is a musician and asks if his rococo-playing ensemble can use her root cellar as a rehearsal space. She agrees, but unbeknownst to her, Prof. Dorr's "musicians" are actually a motley crew of petty criminals plotting to rob the nearby riverboat casino.

Dorr and his cronies dig a tunnel from Ms. Munson's basement to the money-counting room of the casino and manage to pull off the caper. But Ms. Munson discovers their plans, and when she threatens to go to the police, they plan to kill her. But doing away with Ms. Munson is not as easy as it seems. In the end, through their bumbling and greed, Dorr and his band of miscreants wind up dead. Ms. Munson is left with the stolen money, which she donates to her favorite charitable cause—Bob Jones University.

THE TREES

Perhaps the most consistently (and perhaps unjustly) maligned of the Coen brothers' films, *The Ladykillers* is far from the most theologically or metaphysically satisfying of the filmmakers' cinematic storytelling efforts. Still, there are many gems of spiritual insight beneath the facade of this slapsticky crime escapade.

Unique at the time as the only one of the brothers' films that did not begin with an original screenplay of the Coens' creating, *The Ladykillers* is a retelling of the breezy 1955 comedy directed by Preston Sturges. Set in working-class England, the original *Ladykillers* starred Alec Guinness and Peter Sellers as petty criminals who conspired to pull off the heist of a bank train but were derailed by a sweet pensioner who rents out a room to Guinness and his would-be band of thieves in her old, crooked (literally) home.

The Coens' updated version sets the story in the Bible Belt of the Deep South—in Biloxi, Mississippi. The heroine is the pious if not-so-sweet African-American church lady Marva Munson (Irma P. Hall). Her unlikely nemesis is the eccentric literary professor Goldthwait Higginson Dorr III (Tom Hanks), who darkens her door one "camellia-scented morn" looking to rent a spare room in her house and use her root cellar as a rehearsal space for his alleged rococo musical ensemble.

Dorr is a strange character, dressed anachronistically in a three-piece dust-colored suit, hand-looped bow tie and caped topcoat. He looks like a cross between Mark Twain and his hero, Edgar Allan Poe, with a sinister widow's peak and goatee tempered by a set of goofy, crooked buckteeth and a nervous giggle. From the get-go, Ms. Munson is suspicious of him and his intentions, with good cause. As it turns out, Dorr is plotting a daring heist from the vault of the nearby casino, the *Bandit Queen*, and plans to tunnel from Ms. Munson's cellar to the safe house with the help of a crew of misfits he dubs his "merry little ol' band of miscreants."

Miscreants might be a bit of an overstatement — *ship of fools* is more like it. Dorr finds his coconspirators through a want ad in the *Memphis Scimitar* newspaper. They are Gawain MacSam (Marlon Wayans), a foulmouthed, lecherous janitor on the *Bandit Queen*; Garth Pancake (J. K. Simmons), a jack-of-all trades with a life partner named Mountain Girl and a bad case of irritable bowel syndrome; The General (Tzi Ma), a Vietnamese military man skilled in tunneling who runs the local Hi-Ho Donut (and Croisants [*sic*]) shop; and Lump Hudson (Ryan Hurst), a mouth-breathing simpleton from the local high school football team who, as Dorr describes him, is "the goon, the hooligan, the dumb brute whose actions must be directed by a higher intelligence." Each man is more bumbling than the next and their collective dim-wittedness and infighting lead to the failure of their caper and their sad, if comical, demise.

The film opens on a bridge over the mighty Mississippi River, with the camera trained on a raven sitting atop a gargoyle depiction of a scythe-carrying reaper. As an enormous barge carries refuse to a garbage island in the distance, a gospel song plays — "Come Let Us Go Back to God" by the Soul Stirrers. Throughout the film, the soundtrack of vintage gospel tunes, hymns, and a few rap songs compiled by the music producer T-Bone Burnett (who was also the music archivist for *O Brother, Where Art Thou?*) acts as a kind of omniscient narrator, telling if not the plot itself then the spiritual import behind what occurs onscreen.

Early on, the scene changes to a small, brick police station where Sheriff Wyner (George Wallace) and his Barney Fife-esque deputy (John McConnell) are taking snoring naps while the police scanner registers nothing and a skeleton key hangs tethered to a cobweb next to the single, empty jail cell. Ms. Munson arrives, startling the sheriff and deputy out of their reveries, to complain about a neighbor, Weemack Funthes (Jason Weaver), who has gone down to the Costco in Pascagoula and returned with a boom box. "He been playin' that music—loud!" she cries. " 'Left My Wallet in El Segundo.' Hippity-hop music. You know, they calls it hippity-hop music, but it don't make me want to go hippity hop."

Weemack's loud music, she says, is also disturbing Othar, her long-deceased husband, whose frowning portrait hangs over her fireplace. "And sheriff, do you know what they call colored folk in them songs? Have you got any idea? Niggaz! Two thousand years after Jesus! Thirty years after Martin Luther King! In the age of Montel! Sweet Lord-a-mercy, izzat where we at?"

Ms. Munson wants the sheriff to have a word with Weemack, to "extend that helpin' hand," she tells him. "Don't wanna be tried and found wantin'," she says and mentions something from Scripture that the sheriff can't understand. "Mene, mene, tekel, parsin," she says, quoting a passage from the biblical book of Daniel where supernatural writing on a wall, inscribed by God, foretells the impending downfall of the pagan Babylonian empire. "Don't want that writin' on the wall. Feast a Balthazar! John the apostle said, 'Behold, there is a stranger in our midst come to destroy us!' "

With that, Ms. Munson totters out the door and walks home, where she lights a candle and has a (one-sided) conversation with Othar about Weemack, telling him, "That boy hangin' by a thread over the pit—fiery pit!" Unlike Marge Gunderson in *Fargo*, who represented a moral anchor and a prophetic voice of grace, Ms. Munson is the voice of judgment. Marge functioned, theologically speaking, as "Christ transforming culture," while Ms. Munson clearly demonstrates Niebuhr's "Christ against culture" model, seeing the world as a corrupt and dying place full of treachery and backsliding, hanging by a gossamer thread over the fiery pit, to quote the early American preacher Jonathan Edwards's famous sermon "Sinners in the Hands of an Angry God."

While Ms. Munson is talking to Othar about Weemack, a strange wind blows, making the candles on the mantel flicker. The doorbell rings, and Ms. Munson's cat, Pickles, arches her back and hisses. The caller is Professor Dorr, who manages to let Pickles escape past him when Ms. Munson opens the door. Before she can even ask who he is or what he wants, she orders the professor to climb the tree in her front yard to retrieve the cat. He balks at first, but when she says she'll have to call the police to rescue the cat, he quickly scrambles up the tree to pursue the hissing cat, and he falls to the ground when the branch he's climbed out onto breaks.

We likely are meant to understand Pickles the cat in a mythological sense, as a protector of the home and—as cats were thought of by the ancient Egyptians and others—a higher being from the spirit world that sees things beyond the reach of human understanding. Pickles is immediately hostile toward the professor because he represents evil and threatens the household.

Back in Ms. Munson's parlor, the loquacious Dorr introduces

himself formally and with great flourish, as "Professor Goldthwait Higginson Door III, PhD." "What, like Elmer?" the unpretentious church lady says, frowning.

Dorr: "Beg your pardon, ma'am."

Ms. Munson: "Fudd?"

Dorr: "No no. PhD is a mark of academic attainment. It is a degree of higher learning bestowed, in my case, in recognition of my mastery of the antique languages of Latin and Greek. I also hold a number of other advanced degrees, including the baccalaureate from a school in Paris, France, called the Sorbonne."

Ms. Munson: "Sore bone, well I guess that's appropriate. You ever study at Bob Jones University?"

Dorr: "I have not had that privilege."

Ms. Munson: "It's a Bible school, only the finest in the country. I send them five dollars every month."

Dorr: "That's very gener—"

Ms. Munson: "I'm on their mailing list. I'm an Angel."

Dorr: "Indeed."

Ms. Munson: "They list my name in the newsletter, every issue. I got the literature here, you wanna examine it."

Bob Jones University is a fundamentalist Protestant school in Greenville, South Carolina, notorious for its racist policies. African-American students were refused admittance until 1971, and up until 2000 interracial dating between students was strictly forbidden. Why Ms. Munson holds Bob Jones in such high regard is a mystery. Perhaps she is unaware of its racial politics, and knows it only by its reputation as a conservative Bible school.

Dorr is polite but dismissive of her academic affiliation, such as it is, and Ms. Munson sees right through him, the frown returning to her face. She shows Dorr the room to let, and while looking at the room, he asks her whether she might have a root cellar he could use for his Renaissance/rococo ensemble rehearsals. As he's talking, he notices a print of the Last Supper above the bed and clearly tailors what he says next to appeal to his landlady's spiritual predilections. "We play music that was composed to the greater glory of God. Devotional music. *Church* music," he says. "Gospel music?" Ms. Munson asks, smiling. "Well, inspired by the gospel certainly," he answers, allaying her fears, at least temporarily. It isn't clear whether her suspicion is particularly aimed at Dorr or is the way she greets every new person in her life.

After we are introduced to the "merry little ol' band of miscreants" in a series of comical vignettes, our next stop is a Sunday morning service at Ms. Munson's white-clapboard Baptist church. In one of the highlights of the film, the church choir (played by the real-life Abbot Kinney Lighthouse Choir, Rose Stone, and the Venice Four) performs a rousing rendition of "Let Your Light from the Lighthouse Shine on Me" before the rotund pastor delivers a classic sermon based on Scripture from the book of Exodus:

> I know you all remember that when Moses came down the mountain carrying the word of God, come down that Sinai peak, he caught them Israelites red-handed. What'd he catch 'em doin'? He caught 'em worshippin' a golden calf. He caught 'em worshippin' a false god. He caught them Israelites in decline. In decline!
>
> What did Moses do when he saw those declinin', backslidin', never-mindin' sinners? What did he do? Moses smote those sinners in his wrath! Yes, he did! Y'all know what "smote" is? I smite, you smite, he smites, we done smote! To smite is to go

upside the head! Because sometimes, brothers and sisters, that's the only way! The only way.

To smite is to remind we got to stop that decline and scramble back up to the face of the Almighty God! Instead of worshippin' that golden calf, that earthly trash on that garbage island. That garbage island in the shadowland, wa-a-ay, way outside the kingdom of God! That garbage island, where scavenger birds feast on the bones of the backslidin' damned. And so, let us pray.

The scene painted by the pastor's sermon evokes the image of the literal garbage island in the middle of the river in town, where four of the five "merry little ol' band of miscreants" (and Mountain Girl) will find their unfortunate final resting place. And the sermon is obviously on Ms. Munson's mind when she slaps the snot out of MacSam for cussing in her basement, telling him, "This is a Christian house, boy! None of that hippity-hop language in here! I'm trying to help you better yourself, boy!" (MacSam's appearances on screen are often accompanied by songs from the rap group Nappy Roots. As he wheels his janitor's cart through the casino, the Roots sing, "Trouble here, trouble there ... the devil's in this world.") As Ms. Munson lands another smack upside McSam's head, she adds, "Sometimes it's the *only* way!"

Against all odds and with not a few mishaps — for example, Pancake blows off one of his fingers by hitting a block of plastic explosives with a hammer during a "safety meeting" — Dorr and his band of idiots manage to pull off the $2.6 million casino heist while Ms. Munson is at church, where the choir sings, "Soon we'll be done with the troubles of this world ..."

But when the explosives fail to detonate and destroy the tunnel they've dug between Ms. Munson's root cellar and the casino's counting room, Pancake taps the detonator with his Leatherman tool until it resumes its countdown with only thirteen seconds left. He scrambles back down the tunnel toward the cellar where Dorr and the others are counting the stolen money and just about reaches the opening when the bomb explodes, blowing him into the room and sending the bills flying. Ms. Munson, who has returned early from church to prepare tea for some of her church friends, goes to the basement to see what's happened and catches the thieves red-handed.

Dorr attempts to calm Ms. Munson down, telling her a story that appeals to her moral stand against the evils of gambling and explaining that the casino's insurance policy will cover the loss at the expense of only one penny to each of the insurance company's policyholders. "Find the victim, Ms. Munson," he says. "I challenge you. Even the casino itself, that riparian Gomorrah, shall suffer no harm." She momentarily accepts his line of reasoning, until she looks up at Othar's frowning portrait (in a whimsical touch, the Coens' change the painting's expression depending on what's happening in the plot) and once again finds her moral center. She gives them a choice: return the money and go to church with her, or she tells the police. "Engage in divine worship?" Dorr responds, incredulous, to which she says, adamantly, "I've made up my mind. It's church or the county jail!"

Dorr consults with the others, asking the near-silent General, a Buddhist, whether there might be a "middle way." After a few moments of silence, he responds, "Must float like leaf on river of life ... and kill old lady." They foolishly plot to kill Ms. Munson, drawing straws to see who will do the dirty deed. When MacSam chooses the short straw, he creeps upstairs with a gun and a pillow, sneaking up behind Ms. Munson to dispatch her. However, Ms. Munson sees him, seizes the pillow, and attacks him, sending him fleeing back to the basement. When he tells the others he can't do it because she reminds him of his mama, he gets into a scuffle with Pancake and the gun goes off, killing MacSam. The others dump his body from the bridge to one of the ever-present garbage barges headed to the trash island.

Pancake sneaks off with the money, replacing the stacks of bills in a cello case with back issues of *Mother Jones* magazine, but the General catches up with him as he loads the loot into the back of Mountain Girl's van, strangles both of them, and dumps both of their bodies onto yet another barge on the river. The General draws the next short straw, but when he creeps into Ms. Munson's bedroom while she sleeps, tucking his lit cigarette into his mouth (she doesn't allow smoking in the house), a sounding cuckoo clock startles him. He swallows the lit butt, attempts to put it out with water from a glass next to her bed (that contains her soaking dentures), runs from the room, trips over Pickles, and falls down the stairs to his death. Lump and Dorr drop his body onto a passing garbage barge, and the professor orders the big lug that he'll have to kill Ms. Munson.

Lump, who passes for the holy fool in *The Ladykillers*, has an attack of conscience, telling the professor that maybe Ms. Munson is right and that they should give the money back and go to church. When the professor tells his "dumb brute" that if he doesn't kill Ms. Munson, he'll do it himself, Lump, mustering heretofore-unseen gumption, says he "can't allow" that. Dorr, in his one moment of unmitigated anger and vitriol, calls Lump a "very, very, extremely stupid boy." Lump draws the gun on Dorr and pulls the trigger. It doesn't discharge, and, thinking the chambers empty, he points the gun at his face to inspect it and accidentally shoots himself in the head. He tumbles from the bridge and onto a passing garbage barge bound for the trash island.

The professor, thinking himself lucky to be left with the stolen money all to himself, looks up and sees a raven land on the head of the gargoyle. Always the Poe fan, he takes this as a good omen and begins to recite Poe's poem "To Helen." But the raven knocks the head off the gargoyle, which brains Dorr and sends him over the side of the bridge and into the river, where he is strangled by the cape of his topcoat as the gospel tune "Let Your Light from the Lighthouse" begins to play. To end the scene, Pickles appears, dropping Pancake's finger — the last vestige of evil left in the house — off the side of the bridge onto yet another passing garbage barge.

The film ends with Ms. Munson making another visit to the police station to tell the sheriff about the casino heist. The sheriff, busy investigating the missing $2.6 million from the *Bandit Queen*, tries to send her home. She tells him the money is in her basement and begins to tell them the tale of Dorr and his merry band of miscreants. The sheriff and deputy think she's delusional and, humoring her, tell her she can keep the money. "Could I just give it all to Bob Jones University?" she says, smiling broadly. "That'd be nice, ma'am," the sheriff says. "As long as everybody knows," she says, and walks out of the police station toward home, as Blind Willie Johnson begins to sing, "Let Your Light from the Lighthouse Shine on Me."

THE MORAL OF THE STORY...

That light shines equally on the righteous and the wicked, or so St. Matthew tells us in his gospel. Still, the Coens leave unanswered the question of what is the greater good. In *The Ladykillers*, the wages of stupidity—if not sin—is death, and the moral center holds, but the ill-gotten gains from the gambling emporium go to a Bible school with a racist past. Perhaps, as the author of the book of Ecclesiastes writes, it's all vanity, and in the end, blind faith and the folly of humankind win a few.

CHAPTER 12

NO COUNTRY FOR OLD MEN

"You don't know what he thinks."

THE FOREST

While hunting antelope near his trailer home in rural Texas, Llewelyn Moss stumbles across the aftermath of a drug deal gone wrong—a gruesome scene of mass murder with the bullet-riddled bodies of drug runners lying everywhere. He also discovers a document case with $2 million and foolishly decides to keep it. Meanwhile, cold-blooded killer Anton Chigurh has been dispatched to track down the drug money and quickly picks up Llewelyn's trail. Along the way, Chigurh, whose weapon of choice is the kind of air rifle ranchers use to slaughter cattle, kills indiscriminately and without mercy.

While Chigurh tracks Llewelyn, the laconic local sheriff, Tom Bell, tracks Chigurh and tries unsuccessfully to convince Llewelyn to turn himself in before Chigurh catches him. In the end, Chigurh murders Llewelyn and his young wife, Carla, and gets away, leaving Bell to contemplate his impotence in the face of unchecked violence and pure evil.

THE TREES

Theodicy. It's one of the most confounding theological conundrums of human history—the question that begs to know why, if there is a God and God is good, does persistent evil exist in the world. Of all the theological questions Joel and Ethan Coen have posed during their twenty-five years of filmmaking, the inquiry they make in their Oscar-winning masterpiece *No Country for Old Men* is, perhaps, the most unanswerable and the most distressing, particularly to us modern humans who have often believed that the sheer force of our intellect and the rules of science make nothing unknowable.

In *No Country for Old Men*, by all accounts a painstakingly faithful cinematic interpretation of the Cormac McCarthy novel of the same name, the Coens have created one of the most chilling, uncompromisingly wicked characters in film history, the mass murderer Anton Chigurh (Javier Bardem). Without remorse or any hint of the possibility for redemption, Chigurh kills mercilessly and gleefully. His first kill on film—the brutal strangulation of a young sheriff's deputy (Zach Hopkins) who has arrested him by the side of a rural Texas highway for an unspecified crime—elicits an almost erotically rapturous response from the killer. As he chokes the life from the deputy, who writhes helplessly atop Chigurh, the killer stares wildly heavenward, as if to dare some force of love and righteousness to intervene. When the deputy finally dies, Chigurh exhales with an almost orgasmic satisfaction. His eyes are dead, dark, and fathomless; they sparkle only when he is torturing his victims physically or mentally. He is the embodiment of evil.

In the moral universe of dusty West Texas, Chigurh's righteous counterpart is the laconic sheriff Ed Tom Bell (Tommy Lee Jones), a sixty-something lawman increasingly disillusioned with the brutality and violence he sees in the world. Things are changing for the worse, society is coming apart at the seams, and he is starting to believe it's utterly foolish to try to stop the descent into chaos. Bell begins the film as its narrator, but as the story unfolds in scene after scene of wild violence, the narration stops, as if he has no words for what he's witnessing—as if he's given up any hope of stopping Chigurh's homicidal rampage.

In his opening voiceover monologue, Bell tells us he has been a sheriff since he was twenty-five years old. His father was a sheriff, and his grandfather before that. It's a family tradition he's clearly proud to continue, and he speaks wistfully of a time now long gone, when a lawman knew he could make a difference:

> Some of the old-time sheriffs never even wore a gun. A lot of folks find that hard to believe. Jim Scarborough never carried one. That's the younger Jim. Gaston Boykins wouldn't wear one, up in Comanche County.... You can't help but compare yourself against the old-timers. Can't help but wonder how they would've operated in these times.
>
> There was this boy I sent to the electric chair at Huntsville here a while back. My arrest and my testimony. He killed a fourteen-year-old girl. Papers said it was a crime of passion, but he told me there wasn't any passion to it. Told me he'd been planning to kill somebody for about as long as he could remember. Said that if they turned him out, he'd do it again. Said he knew he was going to hell. Be there in about fifteen minutes. I don't know what to make of that. I surely don't.
>
> The crime you see now, it's hard to even take its measure. It's not that I'm afraid of it. I always knew you had to be willing to die to even do this job. But I don't want to push my chips

forward and go out and meet something I don't understand. A man would have to put his soul at hazard. He would have to say, OK, I'll be part of this world.

Although the film is set in 1980, Bell's forlorn existential questioning has an eerie resonance today, giving a voice to the profound impotence many of us feel in this post–9/11 era where many kinds of previously unthinkable violence now seem possible and even necessary. It is still an open question, however, whether there is anything we can do to restore moral order—to create a world where it simply isn't possible to fly passenger planes into skyscrapers in New York City or for democratic governments to torture in the name of a greater good. Such questions lay in stark relief on the screen of *No Country.*

Chigurh will kill using any means at hand, but his preferred method of execution is a high-pressure air gun that, in a split second, shoots and retracts a metal rod. It's what ranchers use to slaughter cattle. It leaves no shell casings, no spray patterns—just a small, lethal hole. After escaping from the sheriff's station in a squad car, Chigurh uses his weapon of choice to kill a motorist whose car he wants. He could have simply taken the man's car, but he *wanted* to kill.

The man caught in the middle of Chigurh's killing spree is Vietnam veteran Llewelyn Moss (Josh Brolin), who, while hunting antelope on an open range near his trailer home, stumbles across a scene of mass murder—a Mexican drug deal gone wrong. Half a dozen men and their dogs have been slaughtered. A welder by trade, Llewelyn investigates the scene more closely and finds a survivor —mortally wounded but still alive—seated in the cab of a pickup truck. Speaking Spanish, the man asks for water, but Llewelyn doesn't have any. He leaves the man to die and tracks another survivor to a nearby ridge, where, he discovers, the man has died under a tree after he fled the mass-murder scene and sought shelter from the relentless Texas sun. Next to the corpse there is a case full of money, which Llewelyn foolishly decides to take home with him.

Back at the trailer, we meet his wife, Carla Jean Moss (Kelly Macdonald), who quizzes him about where he's been and how he came by the gun he is carrying. "Where'd you get the pistol?" she demands to know. "At the gettin' place," he answers. Lying awake in bed that night, Llewelyn has an attack of conscience and decides to return to the murder scene to bring the lone survivor a jug of water. He knows it's the right thing to do. He also knows it might get him killed, but he goes anyway.

Llewelyn is Everyman. He's not wicked like Chigurh. And he's not a righteous man like Bell either. He's something in between, a complicated man whose free-will choices—both good and bad—ultimately lead to great tragedy for him and those he loves most. Back at the crime scene, Llewelyn finds the survivor dead from a shotgun blast to the head and is quickly surprised by a group of men who clearly have returned to the scene looking for the suitcase of money that's hidden back at the trailer. They pursue him, shooting at him with high-powered rifles and wounding him in the shoulder.

Llewelyn flees on foot into a river, where a pit bull belonging to one of his pursuers chases him like a hound from hell. Llewelyn crawls up onto the shore, reaches for his pistol, and shoots the dog just as it lunges for his head. He returns to the trailer and tells Carla Jean to start packing. He has left his pickup at the murder scene, so he knows that come morning the killers will be looking for him and the money. Wanting to protect his wife, and promising that she'll never have to work another day in her life, Llewelyn puts Carla Jean on a bus bound for Odessa, where her mother lives. He says he'll catch up with her in a few days when it's safe to reunite.

Meanwhile, in the most chilling scene of the entire film, Chigurh stops for gas and a snack at an isolated filling station, where he mercilessly menaces the elderly clerk. When the man makes small talk about the weather, Chigurh calmly taunts him, asking him questions about his life and scoffing when the man said the gas station business once belonged to his wife's family. Chigurh pulls a quarter from his pocket and asks the man, "What's the most you've ever lost in a coin toss? Call it." After protesting that he "didn't put nothing up" in the bet, the man says, "Look, I gotta know what I stand to win." "Everything," Chigurh answers, never taking his crazy eyes off the man. Luckily for him, the man accurately calls "heads," and Chigurh spares him. Chigurh's homicidal rage is random, totally a matter of chance. It doesn't make any sense, which makes it all the more terrifying.

Chigurh turns up at the scene of the mass killing, summoned by a couple of white businessmen who have hired him to track down the missing money. They give him a radio transponder that will sound if he's near the money case. Then he shoots them. Bell and his deputy ride horses out to the crime scene to investigate, and Bell recognizes Llewelyn's truck. He knows that Llewelyn isn't the kind of man to be involved in a drug deal and begins to piece together what's happened, realizing that whoever was responsible for the most recent bout of carnage at this crime scene must be the same man who killed the motorist for his car the day before. Clearly, Bell has an inkling that the man they're looking for is a force to be reckoned with. "It's a mess, ain't it sheriff," the deputy says. "If it ain't it'll do till a mess gets here," Bell answers prophetically.

Chigurh shows up at Llewelyn's trailer, blowing the lock off the door with his air gun. Not finding what he's looking for, Chigurh goes to the trailer park office, still on the hunt for Llewelyn. When the secretary refuses to tell him where Llewelyn works, we're sure he's going to kill her. But then someone flushes a toilet in the next room, and Chigurh leaves.

Bell and his deputy arrive at the Mosses' trailer just moments after Chigurh's departure—a bottle of milk he was drinking is still sweating on the coffee table where he left it. Meanwhile, Llewelyn checks into a hotel on his way to the border town of Del Rio (presumably so he can escape into Mexico) and hides the money case in an air-conditioning vent. He knows he's being stalked, but not by whom. Chigurh, who phones Carla Jean (having discovered her number on a phone bill at the trailer), is on his way to Odessa; and Bell, who has begun to understand that Llewelyn is involved in something way over his head, is trailing Chigurh.

Driving across a bridge on his way to find Llewelyn, Chigurh spots a pheasant perched on the railing and shoots at it. It's an image reminiscent of a far more comical scene in *Raising Arizona* in which Leonard Smalls, the Lone Biker of the Apocalypse, randomly shoots at lizards and tosses hand grenades at bunny rabbits. Unlike Smalls, Chigurh is anything but cartoonish, and his violent outburst toward a helpless animal is haunting rather than hilarious.

Using the radio transponder, Chigurh tracks Llewelyn to his motel. The first room he enters is the wrong one, but he guns down the three men inside without a second thought. From here, the middle portion of the film unfolds in one long, nail-biting game of cat and mouse, as Chigurh chases Llewelyn from one seedy motel to another. Along the way, we're introduced to Carson Wells (Woody Harrelson), who is drafted by the businessman (Stephen Root) who had originally hired Chigurh to now track down Chigurh, who is now regarded as a "loose cannon." "Just how dangerous is he?" the man asks. Wells, dressed in dove gray and a matching ten-gallon hat, responds blithely, "Compared to what? The bubonic plague? He's bad enough that you called me. He's a psychopathic killer, but so what? They're plenty of them around."

Chigurh's murderous rampage continues unabated as he pursues Llewelyn through the streets of Del Rio and across the border into Mexico. He kills a hotel clerk, and then shoots a truck driver who stops to pick up Llewelyn. The two come almost face-to-face in a shoot-out on the street, each man suffering horrific, but not fatal, gunshot wounds. (In a truly disgusting scene, the Coens train their camera unflinchingly on a naked Chigurh as he performs surgery on himself to remove the buckshot from his leg.)

Llewelyn awakens in a Mexican hospital bed, and Wells, holding a bouquet of wilting flowers, is seated in a chair next to him. He's come to warn Llewelyn about Chigurh, saying that there's no way he can escape the psychopath. "He doesn't have a sense of humor," Wells says. "You're not cut out for this. You're just a guy who happened to find those vehicles.... You don't understand. You can't make a deal with him. Even if you gave him the money he'd still kill you just for inconveniencing him. He's a peculiar man. You could even say he has principles, principles that transcend money or drugs or anything like that. He's not like you. He's not even like me."

Bell visits Carla Jean in Odessa and promises to help Llewelyn. "When Llewelyn calls, just tell him I can make him safe," the sheriff says. Sadly, it's a promise he can't keep. Meanwhile, Chigurh finds Wells as he's walking into his hotel and takes him to his room, where he taunts him calmly for a few minutes before killing him. "We don't have to do this," Wells says, offering to tell him where the money is, which Llewelyn tossed off a Del Rio bridge onto the riverbank below. Chigurh continues to goad Wells.

Chigurh: "Let me ask you something. If the rule you followed brought you to this, of what use was the rule?"

Wells: "Do you have any idea how crazy you are?"

Chigurh: "You mean the nature of this conversation?"

Wells: "I mean the nature of you."

Chigurh shoots Wells dead and continues on his hunt for Llewelyn and the missing case of money. We never see the final confrontation between Chigurh and Llewelyn, whose murder occurs offscreen, with Bell arriving at the motel in El Paso just after Chigurh, we presume, has done Llewelyn in. (On his way to kill Llewelyn, Chigurh murders three more men — the businessman who sent Wells after him, a random accountant in that office, and a kindly farmer who stops to help him jump-start his car.) Before his death, Llewelyn has a phone conversation with Chigurh, who tells him he plans to kill Carla Jean, but won't if Llewelyn brings him the money. "I won't tell you you can save yourself because you can't," Chigurh says. Llewelyn declines his offer. It's a tragic choice.

Bell has a conversation with the sheriff in El Paso, who bemoans the out-of-control violence that Chigurh represents, saying "How do you defend against it?" Bell, who says he sometimes thinks Chigurh is just a ghost, goes to visit his uncle Ellis (Barry Corbin), a retired sheriff who is confined to a wheelchair (having been shot by a crime suspect some years before) and lives in a ramshackle house that he shares with a dozen feral cats. Bell's wife, Loretta (Tess Harper), has told Ellis that Bell intends to retire, and he wants to know why. "I feel overmatched," he says. "I always thought when I got older, God would sort of come into my life in some way. He didn't. I don't blame him. If I was him I'd have the same opinion about me that he does."

Ellis quickly retorts, "You don't know what he thinks."

Chigurh, meanwhile, is waiting for Carla Jean when she returns home from her mother's funeral. (Her mother, we presume, has died of the cancer she complained of in an earlier scene.) She knows who he is and what he's come to do. "You got no cause to hurt me," she says. "No, but I gave my word," he says. He offers to toss a coin for her fate. "Call it," he growls. "No. I ain't gonna call it. The coin don't have no say. It's just you," she says, before he executes her offscreen.

Chigurh calmly walks out the front door of Carla Jean's mother's house, gets into her car, and drives away, headed toward an intersection where, we see, the light has just turned green. In a twist that in another, less bleak story might have been an instance of *deus ex machina*, a station wagon plows into the side of Chigurh's car. He emerges, bloodied and broken with a bone sticking out of his arm, but alive. Two teenage boys on bikes approach him, and Chigurh offers one of them money for his shirt. "Hell, mister, I'll give you my shirt," the boy says, literally handing him the shirt off his back. Chigurh cannot accept this altruistic act and insists the boy take a hundred dollar bill from him. We see that he's managed to corrupt the boys, who argue over how to split the money. As the killer limps away through the otherwise sunny, peaceful suburban streets, viewers may recall the line from *The Ladykillers*, where Marva Munson quotes St. John: "Behold, there's a stranger in our midst come to destroy us."

The film ends with a breakfast scene at Bell's house. He's retired now and clearly a little lost. His wife asks him how he slept, and he says he had dreams. She prods him to tell her what they were, and he says there were two—and his father was in both. He doesn't remember much about the first, but his recounting of the second serve as the film's final words before the screen goes black:

> It was like we was back in older times and I was on horseback goin' through the mountains at night, goin' through this pass in the mountains. It was cold and there was snow on the ground and he rode past me and kept on goin'. Never said nothin' goin' by. Just rode on past, and he had his blanket wrapped around him and his head down, and when he rode past I seen he was carryin' fire in a horn the way people used to do, and I could see the horn from the light inside of it. 'Bout the color of the moon. And in the dream I knew he was goin' on ahead and that he was fixin' to make a fire somewhere out there in all that dark and all that cold. And I knew that whenever I got there, he would be there. And then I woke up.

THE MORAL OF THE STORY . . .

Many viewers were stumped by *No Country for Old Men*, not knowing quite what to make of this seemingly hopeless story that was such a departure from the rest of the Coens' work. At first, I wondered whether Chigurh, like Leonard Smalls, wasn't simply the ghost that Bell thinks he might be, a projection of the good sheriff's worst fears of helplessness in the face of encroaching evil—a force he was simply unable to stop or defend against. Yet, as the film brings home with brutal clarity, Chigurh is undeniably real. He is not simply a specter, but a living nightmare, evidence for what humanity can become if ruled only by greed, aggression, and a twisted, myopic sense of justice.

In this bleakest of their films, the Coen brothers shine a light on the darkness, looking evil square in the face without blinking. They're not afraid to ask the theodicy question about the nature of evil and the goodness of God, a question as old as humankind. And they are brave enough to leave it unanswered.

CHAPTER 13

BURN
AFTER READING

"We don't really know what anyone is after."

THE FOREST

Osbourne "Ozzie" Cox, an expert analyst on the CIA's Balkans desk, is demoted unceremoniously from his position at "the Agency," so he decides to quit and write his memoirs. Ozzie's wife, a cold pediatrician named Katie who barks at her terrified young patients, wants a divorce. Katie expects her lover, Harry, a federal marshal (who hasn't discharged his sidearm in twenty years of service) and serial philanderer, to leave his wife, who is a children's book author. But Harry's wife, who's also cheating, leaves him first.

In a different part of town, a disc with Ozzie's CIA memoirs winds up on the locker room floor of Hardbodies gym. Two hapless gym employees—Chad and Linda—mistakenly believing it to contain high-level spy secrets, try to blackmail Ozzie so Linda can foot the bill for the plastic surgery she's convinced she needs to "reinvent" herself. Ozzie's rage, Harry's philandering, and the CIA's own bumbling all have disastrous—and deadly—consequences.

THE TREES

Id•i•o•cy \ ì-dē-ə-sē \ *n. pl.* **-cies** (ca. 1529) 1 : utterly senseless or foolish behavior; a notably stupid or foolish act, statement, etc. 2 : *Psychol.* the state of being an idiot.

In the moral universes created by Joel and Ethan Coen, idiocy is perhaps the one unforgivable sin. Nothing incurs the unmitigated wrath of the Coen brothers like utter stupidity. Set in modern-day Washington, D.C., among the denizens of the so-called "intelligence community," *Burn After Reading* could well have been titled *A Confederacy of Dunces*.

Idiocy is not, of course, one of the classic seven deadly sins. And in the Jewish tradition, there is no such thing as an unforgivable sin. The Torah teaches that humankind's ability to sin never surpasses God's capacity to forgive (see Exodus 34:6–7). That said, there are three sins one is never, ever supposed to commit: idolatry, murder, and adultery.

As the plot of *Burn After Reading* unwinds, the major characters manage to cover all seven deadly sins and commit each of the three big no-no's of idolatry (in this case, worshiping at the altars of money, power, and vanity), murder, and adultery. While they are punished for these sins—in the Coeniverse every action has a reaction and no bad deed goes unpunished—they may indeed find forgiveness for them. Their flagrant stupidity, however, remains their one fatal, irredeemable flaw.

Like so many of the Coen brothers' earlier films, *Burn After Reading* opens with a long shot—a cosmically long shot, for that matter, taken from a satellite in outer space. First we see planet Earth as a whole, then the shape of continents and, as the camera zooms closer still, the passel of CIA buildings in Langley, Virginia, and lastly a close-up of a man's oxford shoes as he walks briskly down a nondescript hallway.

A door opens and we see that the shoes belong to Osbourne "Ozzie" Cox (John Malkovich), a veteran analyst at the CIA, who has been summoned to meet with his superior and, much to his surprise, two other agency wonks. Ozzie's boss, Agent Palmer (David Rasche), tells Ozzie he's been removed from his position on the Balkans desk and moved to a lower-security clearance job in the State Department. Without giving himself even a few seconds for the news to sink in, Ozzie immediately reacts. "What the f–is this?" he howls. "Is it my—I know it's not my work. I'm a great f–ing analyst."

"You have a drinking problem," Agent Peck (Hamilton Clancy) interrupts. Ozzie recoils slightly, stares at Peck and repeats, "I have a drinking problem." Then Ozzie erupts again: "This is an assault. I have a drinking problem? F–you, Peck, you're a Mormon. Next to you we all have a drinking problem. Whose ass didn't I kiss? Let's be honest! This is a crucifixion! This is political! Don't tell me it's not." With that, Ozzie storms out of the office.

Later that afternoon in the kitchen of their tony brownstone, we meet Katie (Tilda Swinton), Ozzie's stern British wife. While mixing himself a rum and Coke, Ozzie tries to tell Katie about his day, but she's only concerned about the cheeses he's neglected to pick up for their cocktail party that evening. She storms out of the house in a rage, leaving Ozzie sputtering about "bigger news."

At the cocktail party, Harry (George Clooney), a twenty-year veteran of the U.S. Marshal Service, makes awkward small talk with other guests and says he carries a sidearm but has never fired it in the line of duty. Ozzie offers Harry some chevre on toast. At first, Harry recoils, muttering something about having "lactose reflux." Condescendingly, Ozzie corrects him: "You're lactose intolerant? Or you have acid reflux? They're two different things." Katie intervenes, interrupting Harry's wife, Sandy (Elizabeth Marvel), just as she begins to talk about the children's books she writes, and spirits Harry away to the kitchen. "He knows, doesn't he?" Harry stage-whispers to Katie, his lover. "Don't be an ass," Katie snaps. "He doesn't know a thing."

In their car on the way home from the Ozzie party, Harry and Sandy recap the evening. "What a horse's ass," Harry says of Ozzie. "I don't know why we see them," Sandy says. "Well, she's all right," Harry replies. "She is a cold, stuck-up bitch," Sandy retorts. In a later scene, while lying next to each other in the master suite of Ozzie's boat discussing plans to leave their spouses, Katie and Harry have a similar conversation. "Of course, it would be easier for you," Harry says. "Why's that? I don't see that," Katie says. "Well, you know, because he's such a dope. But Sandy, she's a good lady. A very special lady," he replies, nervously. "She's a cold, stuck-up bitch," Katie snaps. It's a matter of perspective, you see. One man's stuck-up bitch is another man's very special lady.

Perspective — or, more specifically, *lack* of perspective — is a recurring theme throughout *Burn After Reading*. When we're introduced to Linda Litzke (Frances McDormand), she's standing partially clothed in a plastic surgeon's office while the doctor uses a felt-tipped marker to highlight her body's slight imperfections. Linda is darling, but she only sees the faults in her trim body. "The Litzkes are big," Linda says. "My mom had an ass that could pull a bus. Father's side too, although Dad tends to carry his weight in front of him.... And what about the face? You know, the window to the soul?"

The plastic surgeon (Jeffrey DeMunn) recommends four separate surgeries: liposuction, a face-lift, breast augmentation, and a nose job. Then he suggests that Linda might want to get rid of the vaccination scar on her upper arm. "Can you counsel me on this?" Linda whines. "I don't know. Is it unsightly? I see it a lot, a bunch of people have it." Some people don't mind it," the doctor says kindly. "Personal taste!"

Linda works at Hardbodies, a gym in Georgetown, where she seems to spend more time looking for possible suitors online than she does actually working. Enter Chad Feldheimer (Brad Pitt), a childlike personal trainer who is absolutely clueless but immensely kind. He loves his job and is jubilant running on the treadmill with his iPod blaring, fists pumping in the air, and a giant goofy grin perpetually decorating his face. (Chad's smiling demeanor stands in sharp contrast to Katie, who only smiles when she's ridiculing someone else. In fact, the only time she laughs in the film is to mock her husband when he tells her his post-CIA plan is to write his memoirs.)

"Loser. Loser! What is this? They should call this Mr. Saggy dot com," Linda says while perusing the latest batch of men who have responded to her online dating profile, while Chad looks over her shoulder with his usual enthusiasm. "Cripes!" Chad says as they scroll through the pictures of ordinary-looking middle-aged men. "Wait, that guy wasn't bad," he says, pointing to the photograph of a bespectacled, unsmiling individual. "That's a Brioni suit!" The fellow in question is a State Department employee named Alan with noticeable hair plugs.

The next day, Linda is on the phone in her cubicle at Hardbodies, arguing with a customer service representative from her insurance company, who tells her that the plastic surgeries she wants to have are elective and won't be covered by the insurance plan. "I'm reinventing myself," Linda says. "It's all approved by my doctor. But madam. This is not—my job involves, you know, public interface...Could I speak to your supervisor please?" When the supervisor denies Linda's claim, she sits at her desk and weeps. Later, Linda goes on a date with the humorless Alan (Michael Countryman), sleeps with him robotically, and then discovers (when she finds a grocery list obviously penned by his wife and tucked into his wallet) that Alan is married. This seems par for the course. She is looking for love in all the wrong places.

In the scene that follows, Manolo (Raul Anaras), the gym custodian, finds a disc on the floor of the women's locker room containing what Chad and Linda believe are top-secret spy files. "It's talking about SigInt and signals and shit. Signals mean code, you know," Chad says. "Talking about like, department heads here, and their names and shit. And then these other files are just, like, numbers. Arrayed. Numbers and dates and numbers—and numbers. I think that's the shit, man. The raw intelligence." As Chad looks through the files on the office computer, growing ever more excited as each unintelligible, number-laden file ticks by, we meet Ted Treffon (Richard Jenkins), the Hardbodies manager. He's freaked out by the presence of the disc and demands that the two get rid of it.

Linda and Ted go to a bar to discuss the disc and Linda's grievances with the insurance company.

Linda: "I need these surgeries, Ted!"

Ted: "You're a beautiful woman! You don't need—"

Linda: "Ted, I have gone just as far as I can go with this body!"

Ted: "I think it's a very beautiful — it's not a phony-baloney Hollywood body."

Linda: "That's right, Ted, I would be laughed out of Hollywood. I have very limited breasts and a ginormous ass, and I have this gut that swings back and forth in front of me like a shopping cart with a bent wheel."

Ted: "You know, there's a lot of guys who'd like you just the way you are."

Linda: "Yeah. Losers!"

Ted: "Well, I don't know. Am I a loser? Lemme tell you something, I wasn't always a manager at Hardbodies."

Ted takes a photograph from his wallet. It's a younger Ted dressed in black clerical robes and a tall black headpiece. "Fourteen years as a Greek Orthodox priest. Congregation in Chevy Chase," he says. "Well jeez, that's a good job," Linda chirps. "What happened?" "It's a long story," he says. "My point is it's a journey." Ted tells Linda that if she doesn't look in her "own backyard" she might miss Mr. Right. This goes over her head, and she continues to hound him about putting in a request for an advance on her salary so she can pay for her plastic surgeries.

That night, Chad visits Linda at her apartment to tell her, giddily, that he's found out who the disc belongs to. "I have this geek friend, Ernie Gallegos! He does computer stuff — hooks up people's computers and programs their VCRs and shit. So he examines the files and he pulls off the digital watermark that tells what computer they were created on.... I also have [Ozzie's] telephone number. Shall we give him a tinkle?" Linda asks why. "Because he's going to wanna know that his shit is secure. You know, he's gonna be relieved. He might even be so relieved he gives us a reward ... like, you know, the Good Samaritan tax, which is not even a tax, really, since it's voluntary."

The two phone Ozzie, who is asleep in bed with Katie. Rather than thank them for finding the disc, he explodes in a litany of profanities and tells them they're in way over their heads. Chad gets flustered, and Linda interrupts him on the phone, shouting back at Ozzie about the "Good Samaritan tax." When Ozzie warns them not to fool with him, Linda says, "You warn us? You warn us? We warn you!" and slams down the phone.

The idea to blackmail Ozzie is planted in their simpleton brains as Linda decides that a payoff from Ozzie would go a long way toward covering the costs of her surgeries. When Ozzie hangs up the phone, Katie presses him about the conversation. He tells her someone's found a disc containing his memoirs and is trying to blackmail him. "Why in God's name would anyone think that's worth anything?" she sniffs.

Linda isn't the only one trolling the Internet for romantic connections. Harry, who is already having one affair with Katie while maintaining a superficially loving relationship with his wife, is a serial infidel who meets women for random sex through an online dating service. Harry goes on a date with a woman he's met on the Internet and sleeps with her. His next date turns out to be Linda. The two hit it off, and Harry, who tells Linda he's in the midst of a divorce, spends the night. At the office the next day, Linda enthusiastically tells Ted about her date with Harry. "What do you really know about this guy?" Ted asks. "I mean, he could be one of those people who, you know, cruises the Internet." "Yeah," Linda says. "So am I!"

In a hilarious scene, Chad meets Ozzie to collect $50,000 in blackmail money. Squinting and trying to look ominously serious while sitting in Ozzie's car, Chad bumbles and repeats, "Appearances can be deceptive." Ozzie explodes at him and punches him in the nose—and Chad opens the door and flees. Linda picks him up in her car and proceeds to chase Ozzie's car, ramming it from behind, before driving straight to the Russian embassy. Linda believes the Russians will be interested in the "secret spy" disc. At the embassy, a perplexed Russian cultural attaché discusses the contents of the disc with them and begrudgingly accepts it to have it analyzed. He asks them to wait, but Linda says she has a date. "The fish has bitten," she tells Chad, convinced that the Russians are their ticket to fortune, and she promises the cultural attaché that they have access to even more files. (They don't.)

While Ozzie has cocktails with a fellow spy, who informs him that Chad and Linda have taken the disc to the Russians, two men approach and ask Ozzie whether he was in the Princeton graduating class of 1973. (Incidentally, Ethan Coen was in the Princeton class of 1979.) The men are process servers and hand Ozzie divorce papers. Ozzie returns home to the townhouse in the rain to find that Katie has changed the locks and put his belongings on the stoop. He leaves in yet another rage and moves into his boat. Meanwhile, Linda decides that in order to get the most money they can from the Russians, they need to find more of Ozzie's spy files, so she dispatches Chad to the Ozzie townhouse. Before Chad goes to the house, though, Linda insists he remove all of his identification from his wallet and cut the tags out of his suit, just in case he's discovered.

While slurping on his ever-present giant tumbler of Jamba Juice, Chad surveys the Ozzie home from his car across the street; when Katie and Harry leave, he smashes a window and breaks in. But before Chad can find what he's looking for, Harry returns from a jog, and Chad hides in the closet of the upstairs bedroom while Harry showers. Harry goes to the closet to get a shirt, sees Chad, draws his gun in a panic, and shoots Chad in the face. When he searches the body and finds no identification, Harry assumes Chad is a spy and that he's being followed. (The audience knows someone is following Harry, but we're not sure who it is. It turns out to be a private investigator hired by Sandy, Harry's wife, who, we learn, is having an affair of her own and plans to file for divorce.)

Back at CIA headquarters, Agent Palmer pays a visit to his boss, Gardner Chubb (J.K. Simmons), to tell him that the Russians have Ozzie's computer disc, that Chad and Linda plotted to blackmail Ozzie and approached the Russian government with the disc, that Harry has been having an affair with Katie and Linda, and that Harry has killed Chad in Ozzie's house.

Palmer: "Our man surveying hears a gunshot, sees the guy wrestle something into his car, follows him; he dumps the body in the Chesapeake Bay."

Chubb: "Well, what'd he do that for?"

Palmer: "Don't know, sir."

Chubb: "Oh for Christ's sake. Anyone fish the body out?"

Palmer: "Mmm, hmm."

Chubb: "Russian? American?"

Palmer: "Don't know. Scrubbed of ID."

Chubb: "And this—Linda?"

Palmer: "Linda Litzke."

Chubb: "She's Treasury?"

Palmer: "No. We're, um, fuzzy on her."

Chubb: "Well, so we don't really know what anyone is after."

Palmer: "Not really, sir."

Chubb: "This analyst, ex-analyst, uh."

Palmer: "Cox."

Chubb: "Yeah. What's his clearance level?"

Palmer: "Three."

Chubb: "OK. OK. No biggie. For now just keep an eye on everyone, see what they do."

Palmer: "Right, sir. And we'll interface with the FBI on this, uh, dead body?"

Chubb: "No! No. We don't want those idiots blundering around in this. Burn the body. Get rid of it. And keep an eye on everyone, see what they do. Report back when, um, I don't know. When it makes sense."

Realizing that Chad has disappeared, Linda thinks the worst and panics. When the Russian attaché calls her at the Hardbodies office, she asks him whether they "have" Chad—"Did he go over." The attaché is clearly flummoxed, and Linda says she's coming to the Russian embassy to discuss it. At the embassy, the attaché tells Linda they don't know where Chad is. "Well, he was gathering information for you when—" Linda says. "We're not interested in such 'information.' It was drivel," the attaché says. When Linda balks, he has her thrown out.

Meanwhile, back on his boat, Ozzie discovers that Katie has cut off his credit cards and emptied their bank accounts. He trashes the boat in a rage. Back at Hardbodies, Linda tells Ted about Chad's disappearance and their plot to blackmail Ozzie, then asks Ted to break into Ozzie's house to look for information to help get Chad back. "What do you mean, 'get him back'?" Ted asks. "Information is power, Ted! Hel-lo!" Linda snaps. When Ted suggests she go to the police, she erupts tearfully, saying, "I need a can-do person, Ted.

I hate your negativity! I hate all your reasons why not! I hate you! I hate you!" she screams and storms out, leaving Ted crestfallen and, it would seem, resigned to doing her bidding.

Linda has also asked Harry for help finding Chad, and he says he has friends in the intelligence community who should be able to help. When she meets Harry for a date the following day and gives him the address of the last place Chad was seen—Ozzie's house—Harry flips out, thinking Linda is a spy. "Who are you?" Harry growls. "Who are you? The CIA? NSA? The military? Who do you work for? Who do you work for?" he shouts, shaking her by the shoulders. "Who are you?!" he repeats manically. "I'm just Linda Litzke," she says cheerfully, and Harry takes off running.

Ozzie decides to break into his old house to take some of his belongings and discovers Ted in the basement office, looking through his computer files. Gun drawn, Ozzie says menacingly, "And you are my wife's lover?" "No," Ted says, terrified. "Then what are you doing here?" Ozzie recognizes Ted from Hardbodies, where he'd gone a few days before, looking for information about Linda. "I'm not here representing Hardbodies," Ted says. "I know very well who you represent," Ozzie retorts, "You represent the idiocy of today." "I don't represent that either," Ted says. But Ozzie is undeterred: "You're in league with that moronic woman. You're part of a league of morons. Yes. You're one of the morons I've been fighting all my life. My whole f—ing life. But guess what? Guess what? Today, I win," he says and shoots Ted in the shoulder. Ted bolts up the stairs, and Ozzie follows him out the door and onto the street, where he attacks him with a hatchet, killing him offscreen.

In the final scene of the film, we're back in Chubb's office, where Agent Palmer brings him up to speed. Harry has been detained at the airport, where he was attempting to board a plane to Venezuela. A CIA agent who had been following Ozzie saw him attack Ted with the hatchet and, feeling he needed to step in, shot Ozzie. Ozzie is in a coma but isn't expected to pull through. The only loose end is Linda Litzke.

Chubb: "Where is she?"

Palmer: "We picked her up. We have her."

Chubb: "Can we, uh —"

Palmer: "She, she, she says she'll play ball if we pay for some — I know this sounds odd — some surgeries she wants. Cosmetic surgery. She says she'll sit on everything."

Chubb: "How much?"

Palmer: "There were several procedures. All together they run to, um —"

Chubb: "Pay it. . . . What did we learn, Palmer?"

Palmer: "I don't know, sir."

Chubb: "I don't f–ing know either. I guess we learned not to do it again."

Palmer: "Yes sir."

Chubb: "Although I'm f–ed if I know what we did."

Palmer: "Yes, sir. Hard to say."

In the end, the only person who gets what she wants is Linda Litzke. Bumbling, simplistic, and myopic about her own sense of self-worth and the big picture, at least Linda is focused. She wants to reinvent herself. She wants four plastic surgeries that she doesn't need. But she's clear about what she wants, and that sets her apart from the rest of the characters in the film. None of them have any real perspective on what's true, right, important, serious, or enduring. They're lost in their own idiocy, and that is their undoing — their singularly unforgivable sin. But we're left to presume that even when she gets what she wants—a cosmetically orchestrated reinvention—Linda still will be left feeling unfulfilled, lonely, and perhaps riddled with guilt when she realizes her costly reinvention has been, ultimately, only skin-deep.

THE MORAL OF THE STORY ...

The Bible says that in this life, we see through a glass darkly. None of us have God's perspective on ourselves, our actions, or the true meaning of life. None of us see with God's eyes looking down on the world (from outer space, according to some folks) with a mixture of divine joy and sadness.

While ridiculously comical, *Burn After Reading* is a sobering tale about what happens when we don't follow God's laws. It belongs in much the same tradition as the biblical stories of King David, King Saul, and Judas Iscariot—men felled by sins of wantonness, wrath, and greed. The title of the film could be accurately interpreted as a description of what humankind has done with God's Word. Scripture shows us the best possible way to live—unselfishly, lovingly, humbly, and by grace alone. But most of us have, essentially, burned it after reading, discounting the rules of morality in favor of our own stupid, shortsighted desires.

A SERIOUS MAN

CHAPTER 14

A SERIOUS MAN

"What does it mean?"

—

When the truth is found to be lies
And all the joy within you dies,
Don't you want somebody to love?
Don't you need somebody to love?
Wouldn't you love somebody to love?
You better find somebody to love.
"Somebody to Love," Jefferson Airplane

THE FOREST

Set in the Coen brothers' real-life hometown of St. Louis Park, Minnesota in 1967, *A Serious Man** tells the story of Larry Gopnik, a modern-day Job—or so he believes. Gopnik is a physics professor at the local university. His otherwise staid world begins to unravel when his wife, Judith, tells him she's leaving him for another man, a rival professor—the corpulent, pious Sy Ableman. Gopnik's teenage children, Danny and Sarah, are typical teenagers, bored with their suburban lives and stealing money from their parents. Danny, who is about to be bar mitzvahed, uses his ill-gotten booty to buy marijuana. Sarah is saving for a nose job.

---

*Releasing October 2009.

A series of minor calamities has Gopnik questioning the existence of God and the meaning of life. He turns to three rabbis in search of answers to his questions, only to find them unanswerable.

THE TREES (SPOILER ALERT)

Joel and Ethan Coen's fourteenth feature film, *A Serious Man*, is easily the most overtly religious and perhaps the most autobiographical of all of their films. It is set in the late 1960s, when the filmmakers were both teenagers, and in their hometown, a largely Jewish suburb of Minneapolis—St. Louis Park. The story takes place among a community of university professors; the Coens' parents were both professors as well.

An early version of the screenplay and interviews with one of the film's lead actors reveal a deeply personal meditation on the meaning of life and the nature of God. Like many of their films, *A Serious Man* probes grave existential and theological questions without giving any clear answers. And that, the filmmakers seem to be saying, is the point.

Before delving into the milieu of 1967 suburban Minneapolis, the opening scene—conducted entirely in Yiddish—begins with a quote from the eleventh-century French rabbi Rashi. The white letters appear on a black screen: "Receive with simplicity everything that happens to you." The scene then opens with an aerial shot looking down on a snowy Jewish *shtetl* (small village) in Ukraine. There a man, Velvel (Allen Lewis Rickman) is trundling through the snow with a *valenki* (a horse-drawn carriage), smiling to himself in Yiddish, "What a marvel, what a marvel!" as he approaches the cottage he shares with his wife, Dora (Yelena Shmulenson).

Velvel enters the house, and Dora asks him where he's been. He tells her that a wheel came off the cart on his way home from selling geese at the local market. As he struggled to fix the cart, a stranger approached to help him. It was Reb Groshkover (Fyvush Finkel), a kabbalist they both knew from Krakow. "God has cursed us," Dora says. "Groshkover has been dead for three years." Velvel doesn't believe her. "I saw the man! I talked to him!" he says. Dora says her husband must have encountered a *dybbuk* (a ghost) because Groshkover died of typhus at the home of someone she knows.

Suddenly, there's a knock at the door. It's Reb Groshkover. Velvel happily welcomes the aged rabbi and offers him some soup, but Groshkover refuses, saying it's too late to eat. Dora takes this as an affirmation that their visitor is indeed a *dybbuk*—surely ghosts don't eat. When Dora tells Groshkover she believes he's an evil spirit, he laughs good-naturedly. Dora stabs Groshkover with an ice pick. When he doesn't immediately keel over, again she takes this as proof that the visitor is actually a ghost.

"One does a *mitzvah* [good deed] and this is the thanks one gets," Groshkover says and stumbles out of the cottage, disappearing into the night. "We are ruined," Velvel wails. "Nonsense, Velvel," Dora retorts, "Blessed is the Lord. Good riddance to evil."

Maybe Groshkover was a *dybbuk*. Or maybe he was an old holy man whom Dora has just murdered. We just don't know. The screen goes black.

We hear the next scene before we see it. Jefferson Airplane's song "Someone to Love" blares as the image of an earpiece from a transistor radio slowly fades in. It's resting in the ear of Danny Gopnik (Aaron Wolff), a pubescent boy seated in a Hebrew school classroom. With one eye on the elderly rabbi leading the class, Danny reaches into his pocket and pulls out a $20 bill. The scene then cuts to the inside of another human ear, and we hear a doctor mutter, "Uh-huh." The scene switches back to the Hebrew classroom as Danny hisses at another boy seated nearby.

The scene continues to switch between the doctor's office, where Danny's father, Larry Gopnik (Michael Stuhlbarg), is being examined by the doctor, and the Hebrew school, where Danny is trying to pass the $20 bill to Mike Fagle, who, we later learn, Danny owes for supplying him with a lid of marijuana. Eventually, the old rabbi instructor discovers Danny's radio and confiscates it. Back in the doctor's office, Dr. Shapiro (Raye Birk) tells Larry he's in good health, but that he wants to take a few X-rays just to be sure.

Next we see Larry in a university classroom writing physics equations on a blackboard while his thoroughly bored students watch listlessly. Later, back in his office in the physics department, Larry encounters a Korean student named Clive who has come to complain about his failing grade on a midterm exam. Clive is a scholarship student and needs to maintain a certain grade point average to stay in school. He asks Larry to change his grade or allow him to take another exam. Larry refuses. "If I receive failing grade, I lose my scholarship and feel shame," Clive says. "I understand the physics. I understand the dead cat."

The "dead cat" is Schrödinger's cat, a theory of quantum mechanics that presents a paradox: there's a cat in a box with a vial of poison; the cat is either dead or alive, depending on a previous random event. Schrödinger theorized that at some point the cat is equally alive and dead at the same time. Schrödinger didn't mean this hypothesis to be taken literally; he used the dead cat scenario as a thought experiment to illustrate how strange quantum mechanics can be, as well as a kind of litmus test for a person's cognitive strengths and weaknesses, depending on how they interpret the viability of the cat.

"You can't really understand the physics without understanding the math," Larry tells Clive. "The math tells how it really works. That's the real thing. The stories I give you in class are just illustrative; they're like fables, say, to help give you a picture. An imperfect model. I mean, even I don't understand the dead cat." Clive leaves Larry's office somberly, saying, "Very troubling, very troubling." A few moments after he's left, Larry discovers a white envelope on his desk containing $3,000 in bills. He assumes Clive has left it as a bribe.

Larry drives home, and when he enters his house, his wife, Judith (Sari Lennick), and his two children are waiting at the kitchen table. Arthur (Richard Kind), his schlubby, unemployed brother who sleeps on their couch, is locked in the house's lone bathroom, where he passes the bulk of his day draining a sebaceous cyst on the back of his neck with a water-picklike suction device.

After dinner, Judith asks Larry if he's spoken to Sy Ableman (Fred Melamed), a fellow professor and friend of the family. When Larry says he hasn't, Judith proceeds to tell him that she's gotten "very close" to Sy and that she wants a divorce. Larry is completely discombobulated by her news. "What have I done? I haven't done anything!" Larry says. Judith says neither of them have "done" anything, but they've been having trouble for some time and it is what it is. "You always act so surprised. I begged you to see the rabbi," she says. In addition to a civil divorce, Judith also wants a *gett*—a religious divorce—so that she can marry Sy (who is very religious) in the Jewish faith.

Back in his office the next day, Larry confronts Clive about the suspected bribery. Clive neither admits to nor denies leaving the money for Larry. "Actions have consequences," Larry tells him. "Yes, often," Clive says. "Always! Actions always have consequences," Larry shouts. "Not just physics. Morally." Clive answers in his broken English that Larry is "merely surmising" what has happened and leaves the office ominously.

Back at the house, life continues uninterrupted by the drama of an impending divorce. Danny's chief concern is the malfunctioning aerial TV antenna that is interrupting his favorite program, *F Troop*. Sarah (Jessica McManus) is concerned about getting Uncle Arthur out of the bathroom so she can wash her hair before going to the local juice bar. Arthur is preoccupied with his project—writing something called the Mentaculus, which is described as a complex mathematical equation that is supposed to reveal the design (and perhaps meaning) of the universe.

Sy Ableman arrives at the house with a bottle of expensive wine to have a chat with Larry. Sy wants to make sure everything's copacetic between them—that everyone can behave with civility and like adults. Larry doesn't know what to make of Sy's glad-handing and familiarity, particularly when Sy hugs him out of the blue. Later, over cocktails at a local restaurant with Judith in tow, Sy reveals that he thinks it best for Larry to move out of the house so that Danny and Sarah aren't subjected to tensions over the divorce. Sy makes it sound as if he selflessly has everyone else's best interests at heart when, in fact, he's a deeply selfish and manipulative man. Nevertheless, Larry agrees and, at Sy's suggestion, moves (along with Uncle Arthur) into a nearby motel called the Jolly Roger.

Later, back at the university, Arlen Finkle (Ari Hoptman) comes to Larry's office to talk about Larry's candidacy for tenure. Arlen says he doesn't want to alarm Larry, but someone has been sending anonymous letters to the tenure committee making denigrating allegations of "general moral turpitude" against Larry, who assumes the letter writer is his disgruntled Korean student, Clive.

A few days later, Clive's father shows up at the house and confronts Larry in the driveway, claiming the alleged bribery was a cultural misunderstanding. When Larry disagrees, Clive's father threatens to sue Larry for defamation. "Look, it doesn't make sense. Either he left the money or he didn't," Larry says. "Please, accept money," Clive's father responds. "You can't have it both ways!" Larry says. "Why not?" Clive's father answers.

Beset by travails large and small—among other things, Larry is being menaced by an account manager from the Columbia Records Club, who insists Larry is four months behind in payments, even though Larry isn't a member (later it becomes obvious that Danny has applied for membership in his father's name). So Larry turns to family friend Mimi Nudell (Katherine Borowitz) for advice.

Larry: "Everything that I thought was one way turns out to be another!"

Mimi: "Then it's an opportunity to learn how things really are. I'm sorry, I don't mean to sound glib. It's not always easy, deciphering what God is trying to tell you."

Larry: "I'll say."

Mimi: "But it's not something you have to figure out all by yourself. We're Jews. We have that well of tradition to draw on, to help us understand. When we're puzzled, we have all the stories that have been handed down from people to people."

Larry meets with three rabbis, beginning with the junior-most rabbi from the local synagogue, Rabbi Scott (Simon Helberg), who is in his twenties. Larry recounts the dissolution of his marriage and his feeling of being adrift, lost. Rabbi Scott responds:

> I too have had the feeling of losing track of *Hashem* [God]*, which is the problem here. I too have forgotten how to see him in the world. And when that happens, you think, "Well, if I can't see him, he isn't there any more. He's gone." But that's not the case. You just need to remember how to see him.... Because with the right perspective you can see *Hashem*, you know, reaching into the world. He is in the world, not just in *shul* [synagogue]. It sounds to me like you're looking at the world — looking at your wife — through tired eyes.
>
> You can't cut yourself off from the mystical or you'll be — you'll remain — completely lost. You have to see these things as expressions of God's will. You don't have to *like* it, of course.

Larry takes the young rabbi's advice and tries to look at his situation with new eyes. Soon, though, another calamity befalls him. He's in a fender bender, and at the same time Sy is in a fatal car accident. Larry ends up paying for Sy's funeral as a consolation to Judith, who is utterly distraught by her suitor's death. So Larry seeks the counsel of another rabbi, Rabbi Nachter (George Wyner).

"What is *Hashem* trying to tell me, making me pay for Sy Ableman's funeral?" Larry asks. "And did I tell you I had a car accident at the same time Sy had his? The same instant, for all I know. Is *Hashem* telling me that Sy Ableman is me, or we are all one or

---

*Hashem, which literally means "the Name," is the way many traditional Jews refer to God, whose actual four-letter name, YHWH, it is forbidden to pronounce aloud. Even when not speaking Hebrew, many Jews will use the name *Hashem* to refer to God to avoid committing blasphemy.

something?" Rabbi Nachter responds with, "How does God speak to us? It's a good question," and proceeds to tell Larry a long story about a local Jewish dentist, Lee Sussman.

A few years before, Sussman was making a plaster mold of a *goy* (non-Jewish) patient's teeth when he discovered letters etched on the inside of the teeth. The letters spelled out "help me" in Hebrew. Sussman couldn't figure out what it meant. He lost sleep. He started inspecting all of the plaster molds he'd made, looking for more letters —but nothing. Then he decided that the Hebrew letters, which also correspond to numbers, were a sign—a phone number. He called the number, and it rang at a local supermarket. He went to the market looking for more signs but found nothing that made any sense. The puzzle preoccupied him for months; but eventually, the dentist stopped looking for signs, stopped trying to figure it out.

When Larry presses the rabbi for a moral to the story, Nachter tells him, "We can't know everything."

Nachter: "These questions that are bothering you, Larry—maybe they're just like a toothache. We feel them for a while, and then they go away."

Larry: "I don't want it to just go away! I want an answer!"

Nachter: "The answer! Sure! We all want the answer! But *Hashem* doesn't owe us the answer, Larry. *Hashem* doesn't owe us anything. The obligation runs the other way."

Larry: "Why does he make us feel the questions if he's not gonna give us any answers?"

Nachter: "He hasn't told me."

Rabbi Nachter delivers the eulogy at Sy's funeral, heralding the pompous late professor as something of a saint. "Sy Ableman was a man devoted to his community, to Torah study, to his beloved wife,

Esther, until three years ago, when she passed; and to his duty as he saw it," the rabbi says. "Where does such a man go? A *tzadik*—who knows, maybe even a *lamed-vavnik*—a man beloved by all, a man who despised the frivolous? Could such a serious man just disappear?... A frivolous man may vanish without a ripple, but Sy Ableman? Sy Ableman was a *serious* man."

Soon we learn from Judith that Sy was the one writing letters to the tenure committee about Larry. Judith thinks the letters were in support of her husband, but the audience knows differently. If Sy Ableman is a *lamed-vavnik*, one of the thirty-six righteous souls who, according to Jewish mystical tradition, hold the fate of the world on his shoulders, everyone's in a heap of trouble.

Larry attempts to visit the third rabbi, the ancient Rabbi Minda (Alan Mandel), but Minda has retired from pastoral duties and won't see him. At the university, Larry continues to teach, going through the motions but clearly as bored with his own subject matter as his students are. "The Uncertainty Principle. It proves we can't ever really know what's going on," Larry tells his students. "So it shouldn't bother you. Not being able to figure anything out. Although you will be responsible for this on the midterm." One night, Sy Ableman comes to Larry in a dream, wearing a prayer shawl and a yarmulke and seated in his lecture hall.

Sy: "It's clever. But at the end of the day, is it convincing?"

Larry: "Well, yes it's convincing. It's a proof. It's mathematics."

Sy: "Excuse me, Larry. Mathematics is the art of the possible."

Larry: "I don't think so. The art of the possible, that's—I can't remember—something else."

Sy: "I'm a serious man, Larry."

Larry: "I know that. So if I've got it wrong, what do I—"

Sy: "So simple, Larry. See Minda."

Larry: "I know. I want to see Minda. I want to see Minda! They told me that—"

Sy cuts Larry off by grabbing him by the hair and smashing his head into the blackboard, screaming, "See Minda! I f—ed your wife, Larry. I seriously f—ed her! That's what's going on! See Minda!"

Larry tries once again to see Rabbi Minda at the synagogue. "The rabbi is busy," Minda's secretary tells him. Larry can see past her into Minda's office, where the old rabbi is hunched behind an empty desk. "He doesn't look busy," Larry says. "He's thinking," the secretary replies.

A few days later at his bar mitzvah, a stoned, bleary-eyed Danny Gopnik is ushered into Rabbi Minda's office. (Minda was the one who, at the beginning of the film, confiscated Danny's transistor radio.) "When the truth is found to be lies," the old rabbi begins, "and all the joy within you dies—then what?" Danny doesn't respond to the rabbi's recitation of the lyrics from Jefferson Airplane's "Somebody to Love." Minda pulls open the drawer of his desk and hands Danny his radio. "Here—be a good boy."

As the film draws to a close, things seem to be looking up for Larry. Danny has managed to make it through his bar mitzvah. Larry gets word that he'll be tenured. He has the $3,000 to pay his divorce attorney's bill. But then the scene shifts to the inside of the Hebrew school classroom where the instructor announces that there's a tornado warning. Back in Larry's office the phone rings. It's Dr. Shapiro. He wants Larry to come in to talk about the results of the X-rays the doctor took a few weeks back. As Larry drives to Shapiro's office, his car is lashed by torrential rain, the wind howls, the sky darkens, and we hear the roar of an approaching funnel cloud and Grace Slick's voice singing "When the truth is found to be lies ..." as the screen goes black and the credits roll.

THE MORAL OF THE STORY ...

Larry Gopnik is not an evil man. So why do hardships befall him?

Sy Ableman is a scheming, lecherous hypocrite. So why is he celebrated as a righteous, serious man?

What are we supposed to learn when all that we believe is true turns out to be false?

What is the purpose of suffering?

What does God want us to understand?

Can we ever really know what anything means?

The questions posed in *A Serious Man* are as brutal as they are universal. The answers the Coen brothers provide are unsatisfactory, but truthful. There is no quid pro quo with God. We tend to want to take responsibility for the bad things that happen in our lives, but we're not always responsible. We're not in charge. We only get glimpses of the big picture. We want to believe that everything in life is cause and effect because if it's not, that truth — that the innocent will suffer — is too awful to grasp.

Sometimes the righteous suffer and the evil prosper. It doesn't make any sense, and it never will. The filmmakers seem to be saying that we should be good for goodness' sake alone; that life is not about finding answers to the questions we have, but about the living — the journey — itself. What you believe doesn't matter. What matters is how you live.

Live your way to the answers.

THE GOSPEL

CONCLUSION

While marked by murder, mayhem, deception, and all manner of chaos, there is an order—a moral order—to the world depicted in Joel and Ethan Coen's films. That's the good news. The bad news is that when the moral order is upset, the consequences can be dire, brutal, and swift.

The Coeniverse is not a godless place, but the Almighty isn't necessarily a God of mercy and grace. Sometimes God is all about fire and brimstone, retribution, and blind justice. Other times, God seems absent—a clockmaker who winds the watch and walks away. Still other times, God is a projection of our imagination and a representation more of our wants and needs than a real divine force.

Drawing on the theology of their own Jewish upbringing—as well as Christian, Buddhist, and other worldviews they may or may not share themselves—the Coens tackle confounding questions about the meaning of life, the nature of faith and God, and the karmic cycle with equal honesty and aplomb. The result is a complicated gospel—one that, it would seem, the filmmakers want viewers to navigate for themselves rather than showing them the way.

That said, there are certain clear dos and don'ts in the Coeniverse. As Walter Sobchak kindly reminds us in *The Big Lebowski*, "This is not 'Nam.... There are rules."

THE 14

1. What goes around comes around. Even though divine intervention happens from time to time, don't count on it to save you from your sins.

2. Every action has a reaction. What you do has consequences, even if you don't see them immediately.

3. Don't mistreat women. They're all special ladies.

4. Whatever you try to hide, somebody will discover. In other words, your sins will find you out.

5. It is better to be kind than to be right, and love always wins.

6. Take chances. Don't be paralyzed by doubt or fear.

7. Beware of false piety. Sometimes there's a stranger in your midst come to destroy you.

8. Don't get too hung up on dogma and legalism. That's just, like, your opinion, man.

9. All moments might be key moments. Act like they are.

COENMANDMENTS

10. No one knows the quality of a person's heart except for God.

11. When it comes to suffering, don't ask why. There's no good answer.

12. No one ever really knows anyone completely. Remember, you only know what a person chooses to let you know.

13. Be compassionate, respectful, and generous—especially to strangers. You never know when you might be talking to a *lamed-vavnik*, a prophet, or an angel in disguise.

14. You don't know what God is thinking. So quit acting like you do.

Life has many more questions than it has answers. But life isn't about finding all the answers; it's about the journey. So go forth in kindness, with an open mind, a pure heart, and a watchful eye for occasional divine intervention—particularly when you least expect or deserve it.

ACKNOWLEDGMENTS

First and foremost, thank you, Joel and Ethan, for giving us the gift of your films. We are blessed by your artistry and the eternal ideas your films inspire us to consider. I for one can't wait to see what adventures you'll take us on in the years to come.

I am indebted to friends and family—particularly my loving husband, Maurice; my parents, in-laws, and stepkids; and my cherished friends from "the thread"—who have supported and walked with me through the writing of this book and more than humored me while I spent many months immersed in the Coen brothers' august oeuvre. To those of you who suffered through umpteen viewings of *Raising Arizona*, *The Big Lebowski*, *Fargo*, and *The Ladykillers*, when I couldn't stop myself from quoting the dialogue aloud, I ask your kind forgiveness and thank you for your indulgence.

My deepest thanks to the Internet Movie Database; Drew's Script-O-Rama; the purveyors of the websites Coenesque, "You Know, for Kids!" and Dudeism.com; and the urban achievers at Lebowski Fest.

A special word of thanks to my marvelous editor, Angela Scheff, and my beloved agent, Chris Ferebee, for their enthusiasm and unfailing support when I come up with wacky ideas, such as an exegesis of all things Coen.

My sincerest gratitude and appreciation go to Curt Diepenhorst (the world's most creative and lovable designer), Erik Rose for his beautiful artwork, and the rest of the editorial team at Zondervan for helping me to push the envelope.

And, always, thank you, Linda Richardson, for giving me wings.

GROUP STUDY QUESTIONS

1. What is the most spiritual film you've ever seen? Explain why.

2. Which Coen brothers' film speaks the most to you spiritually? Explain why.

3. How can engaging worldviews different from our own enliven our faith?

4. Where do you see a Christian or Jewish worldview or message in the Coen brothers' films?

5. Which Coen brothers' character did you learn most from spiritually? Explain why.

6. Which Coen brothers' film do you believe most accurately depicts the world in which we live? Explain why.

7. Which Coen brothers' film best represents your understanding of God? Explain why.

8. How would you answer the theodicy question from *No Country for Old Men*: If God is a good God, why is there evil in the world?

9. Where do you find similarities between biblical stories and the stories told in the Coen brothers' films?

10. Do you agree with the notion in *Miller's Crossing* that we can never truly know another person? Why or why not?

11. If you had to sit down and have a conversation about faith with one of the Coens' characters, which one would it be? Explain why.

12. After exploring the Coens' fourteen films, what do you think the two brothers make of God?

13. Looking at your life, what decisions have you made or moments have you experienced that seemed trivial at the time but later turned out to be pivotal?

14. What questions do you think the Coen brothers are asking in their films? What answers, if any, do you think they offer?

15. What theological or existential questions would you like to see the Coens explore next?

NOTES

1. Matt Zoller Seitz, "Point Blank: *No Country for Old Men*," November 16, 2007, The House Next Door: *www.thehousenext dooronline.com/2007/11/point-blank-no-country-for-old-men.html* (March 30, 2009).

2. Ethan Coen, "Two Views of Wittgenstein's Later Philosophy," senior thesis, philosophy department, Princeton University, 1979, p. 16.

3. See Luke 8:17; 1 Corinthians 4:5.

4. Dashiell Hammett, *The Glass Key* (New York: Vintage, 1989), 230.

5. Quoted in Andrew Pulver, "Blood Ties," *Daily Mail and Guardian*, August 20, 1998.

6. Ronald Bergan, *The Coen Brothers* (Orion, 2000), 140–41.

7. Ibid, 79.

8. Ibid, 141.

9. Saint Aurelius Augustine, *The Works of Aurelius Augustine, Bishop of Hippo*, ed. Marcus Dodds (Edinburgh: T&T Clark, 1872), 17.

10. Bob Barron, "Fr. Robert Barron Comments on the Movie *Fargo*," You Tube: *http://youtube.com/watch?v=HF8Tm7luxx4* (April 2, 2009).

11. Proverbs 24:16.

12. Oliver Benjamin, "What Is Dudeism?" *http://www.dudeism.com/whatisdudeism.html* (April 3, 2009).

13. Dwayne Eutsey, "The Take It Easy Manifesto," *http://www.dudeism.com/takeiteasymanifesto.html* (April 3, 2009).

Coming August 2010

THE THREAD

FINDING A SACRED PLACE IN CYBERSPACE

CATHLEEN FALSANI

Grace makes beauty out of ugly things.
U2, "Grace"

It began with something wholly unthinkable.

Shortly after 7:00 a.m. one Friday in early April 2008, my husband went upstairs to make us coffee, and I propped myself up in bed, grabbed my laptop, and logged on to Facebook.

There, on the right-hand rail where my friends' status updates pop up randomly, I saw a short sentence that changed my life forever: "David is really sad that Mark died today."

David Vanderveen is a friend of mine from Wheaton College who lives in Laguna Beach, California. I checked the time, realizing it was only 5:00 a.m. on the West Coast, and thought, "Please, God, let him not be talking about Metherell."

Mark Metherell, Dave's best friend, next-door neighbor in Laguna, and all-around partner in crime, was one of my favorite people. A former Navy Seal, Mark was working in the private sector in Iraq helping to train Iraqi forces.

Mark and Dave have notoriously wicked senses of humor, and for a few minutes I thought this must surely be one of their bizarre inside jokes. I sent Dave an email asking—pleading really—for him to tell me he wasn't serious. When I didn't hear back from him immediately, I emailed Mark's other best friend, Dave Burchi, who also lives in Laguna.

"It's not a joke, Cath," Dave wrote back. "Mark was killed by a roadside bomb this morning."

My heart gained fifty pounds and sank in my chest, a painful boulder. By the time my husband returned with our cups of coffee, I was a puddle of tears, sobbing inconsolably as I tried to explain what I'd just learned.

I still can't believe it. Mark, 39, was one of the most alive people I've ever known. He was a year ahead of me at Wheaton, but he stayed for a fifth year to finish a degree in literature (and biology), and we graduated together in 1992. While Mark wasn't one of my best friends, he was certainly one of my favorite friends—ever.

Mark was so many marvelous things. A lanky John Cleese-ian figure swathed in khaki and flannel, he was wryly and riotously funny. Mark could convey more humor with the quiver of one wonky eyebrow than most people can manage with their whole bodies. He was deeply intelligent and wonderfully wacky. An adventurous, sea-loving surfer (even in Lake Michigan), he was literate, faithful, and kind.

And he was a hero to me long before he proudly served his country in the armed forces and beyond. Mark died on April 11, 2008, when the vehicle he was riding in—the lead vehicle in a convoy—struck a roadside bomb outside Sadr City. He was killed instantly, leaving behind his beloved wife, Sarah, their infant daughter, Cora, and a devastated community of friends and family all over the world.

I ached to throw my arms around the heartbroken Daves and the rest of those who knew and loved Mark best. I wanted to tell them what Mark surely would have: that they are loved and treasured for who they are, for the strength and beauty of their spirits, for their wit and friendship, for being the vessels of grace for us that they are.

In those first hours and days after Mark's untimely death, many of us took to the Internet to share stories about our dearly departed friend. It started right there on Facebook, with the dozen or so of us who were already members and the more than fifty who joined to reconnect with old friends so we could grieve together.

One of his former Wheaton roommates told the story I'd long forgotten about the time Mark presided over a particularly raucous off-campus party, seated regally in a thronelike orange chair, completely nude. I shared a few stories of my own, like the time he told me he might join the military so he'd have material for the novel he was writing.

My fondest memory of Mark took place in a dive bar called Punky's not long after we graduated. He didn't engage me in conversation very often (actually I didn't think he liked me very much), but he took me aside in a brotherly fashion to tell me something important. I was about to embark on a new romance, and I don't think he approved of the suitor. Mark said he wanted me to know he thought I too often sold myself short and that I was special. He said I deserved to be cherished by someone who would appreciate all that I am without wanting to change me. Years later, when I met the man who did just that, I had Mark to thank for helping me recognize it.

When I shared that story online, I heard almost immediately from two women I knew at Wheaton. One, Margaret, a distant acquaintance, told me she had a similar conversation with Mark when they were studying in England one summer nearly twenty years earlier. The other was my dear old friend from the college theatre company, Amy, now a massage therapist in Hawaii, whom I hadn't talked to in more than a decade. She posted a note on Facebook saying she remembered the night I came home from Punky's after having that transforming conversation with Mark. She remembered it exactly as I had. That was such a comfort—memory can be a tricky thing—and reconnecting with her after all those years was an enormous blessing.

As we mourned and remembered together in virtual community, one of the words that came up most often in describing Mark was *godly*. By that I think we meant that he embodied all the qualities we like to believe God possesses. Loving. Wise. Patient. Strong. Tender. Surprising. A friend who is listening and watching even when we're not aware of it.

A few days after Mark's death, the Daves set up a memorial website for him where they could catalog all of the stories we were sharing on Facebook for the rest of the world. With Mark's family, they planned a memorial service for him on the beach in Laguna where he spent so many hours atop his board in the surf. They instructed those who were able to attend to please wear flip-flops—Mark's sartorial mainstay that he always called "flippity-floppities."

For those who couldn't make the trip to California, the Daves posted dozens of photographs from the beach service online, accompanied by one of Mark's favorite Grateful Dead songs, "Brokedown Palace," so we could share in the experience from a distance. I wasn't able to travel to Laguna, and the virtual memorial service online was an enormous grace. I must have watched the online slide show a hundred times, crying and laughing at the images, some of them the smiling faces of friends from college I hadn't seen in more than fifteen years.

As the weeks passed, a core group of us continued to "talk" daily on Facebook. Our conversations were about Mark at first, and about faith, loss, God's will, and the grieving process. But they soon turned to broader conversations about our lives, the minutia and the transcendent, bringing each other up to speed on what had transpired in the years since we had all been students at Wheaton.

A couple of weeks after Mark's death, I found myself working on a newspaper column about an event that had recently transpired at our alma mater. One of our favorite professors resigned his tenured position rather than submit the details of his divorce to the scrutiny of a college panel. It was something of a scandal at the time, and I wanted to know what my fellow alumni thought about the situation. So I sent a group email to twenty friends on Facebook, a cross section of men and women with, I surmised, divergent perspectives on life, from the extremely conservative to the wildly liberal.

That email turned into a "thread" that continues to this day, more than six months since Mark went home to be with Jesus. After a few hundred posts, I relaunched the thread under the name "Wine and Jesus: The Communion of Sinnerly Saints," and the increasingly intimate, vulnerable conversation carried on. As of November, the thread is in its sixth incarnation, and we're more than seven thousand posts in.

Like many folks who skew more toward Generation X than Generation Z (for whom the social networking site was, as I understand it, originally intended) I began my foray on Facebook as an exercise in ennui abatement. I went trolling for college and high school friends, more to see how many kids they had and whether they'd lost their hair than for any loftier purpose.

My best friend in St. Louis was on there, and through her I found a few more friends, and so on until I (somehow) amassed upwards of 900 "friends," including some people I actually know, or at least knew once upon a time. It was fun to log on and see who popped up. But it remained little more than a curiosity slaker and awesome time killer until our motley community came together online around Mark's death. Our conversations range from the silly—we spent an entire evening posting our favorite scenes from *Dazed and Confused* and recently had a virtual 1980s dance party, sharing audio and videos of nostalgic dance music (think The Smiths and Flock of Seagulls) from our college days—to the eternal. Grace is a common theme that we come back to time and again, gracespotting, if you will, the hand of God as he reaches into our lives.

We're having the kinds of conversations we used to have when we all lived within walking distance of one another on campus. Except now we're in California and Hawaii, Chicago and New York City, St. Louis and Atlanta, Florida and North Carolina, the United Arab Emirates, the Bahamas, and Spain. Collectively we are husbands and wives; brothers and sisters (in-law and biologically); Protestants, Catholics, and Anglicans; conservatives and liberals; Democrats, Republicans, Libertarians, and Green Party; vegetarians; entrepreneurs; stay-at-home moms; married, divorced, and widowed; mothers and fathers; adopted and adopters; seminary graduates, pastors, and chaplains; writers, filmmakers, artists, and lawyers; church members and church averse; and believers all. Some of us were close friends in college, some of us were acquaintances, and some had never met one another in person. But we are now, I would dare say, utterly and wholly committed to one another. As Bono said in U2's theological opus, "One," "we are one, but we're not the same; we get to carry each other."

A few of us have even begun to rediscover (or exhume) our faith. On Facebook. If you had told me even seven months ago that I would find community—real, authentic, deeply connected, deeply faithful community—online, I would have scoffed at you. I'm not, by nature, a joiner. Had someone created and invited me to join a group of Wheaton grads online to talk about faith and life, I would have declined. But this happened organically, not by design. And here we are, six months of daily interaction later, with a communion of twenty souls all over the world who share our lives, hopes, fears, struggles, and joys together in cyberspace.

We recently had a conversation about how to hard it has been for some of us to reach out, ask for help, and be willing to receive it. *Being merciful to ourselves*, is how Shani, the hospital chaplain, put it. In response, Brian, a filmmaker who is married to Sara, an artist, and who is in the midst of the arduous task of relocating their family (with two very young children) from Los Angeles to Boston, wrote, "Sara and I quote Henri Nouwen frequently of late: 'The weakest among us create community.' Somehow I feel I'm on the receiving end in this thread considerably more often than I am giving out. So thanks to all."

For me, the thread, as we commonly call it, has become what the sociologist Ray Oldenburg, in his book *The Great, Good Place*, described as a "third place." Most people have two primary places—home and the workplace—and then there is a third place where they feel anchored and part of a chosen community. It might be a bar (illustrated beautifully in the television series *Cheers*) or a neighborhood restaurant, a house of worship, or a bowling alley. Wherever or whatever it is, everyone, Oldenburg argues, needs a third place.

Heidi Campbell, a professor of communications at Texas A&M University and author of the book *Exploring Religious Community Online: We Are One in the Network*, has been researching the topic of spirituality and the Internet since 1996. I asked her about my spiritual Facebook experience, and she said it's something she's seeing more and more. Facebook is a kind of "mediated third place that allows people to engage or invigorate their spirituality," she said. "In a contemporary, information-based society, it's often hard to get that face-time connection. It becomes that virtual third place where I can kind of connect with that transcendent part of myself through conversation when I couldn't maybe take the time out to get to church to have it." Or, as is the case with a few of us on the thread, find a physical church where we feel safe enough to have the conversation, as the case may be. On the thread, we're all talking and, more importantly, listening in a way we might not be able to do in person.

We are a group of twenty because that's the limit Facebook puts on the number of people you can have active on a single thread. A few months ago, we talked about starting a regular Facebook group, where the number could be unlimited and anyone could join. But after some discussion, we decided to keep the group as it was — intimate and, frankly, safe. Over time, a few of the original members have drifted out of the thread — too busy to keep up with our frenetic pace of conversation. When we reach a thousand posts, we ask if anyone wants out — to take a break — and if anyone has a suggestion of someone we should invite to the conversation. In all, about thirty-five people have been a part of the thread at one time or another.

"The beauty of Facebook or another online community is that you're choosing your community," Campbell told me. "Because it's a lot of like minds gathering or people with a similar background, like your experience, you can develop a sense of intimacy more quickly. Some criticize that and say it's a false sense of intimacy and a false sense of community because it's self-selecting, homogenous, very tightly bound grounds. But I think you could argue that it's the way you connect with people now. As middle age is staring us in the face, we're trying to reconnect in a lot of ways. There's some part of spirituality that traditional religion doesn't really connect with, but there's that meaning making, that God void, that I want to reconnect with, and so the Internet is becoming a great place, whether it's to explore or to meet other people who are on the search."

I'm not sure which one of us said it first, but somewhere around the second month, we began to refer to the thread as "church." It sure feels like that to us. We've dealt with many of the conflicts that "actual" churches do. There have been misunderstandings, hurt feelings, and arguments over interpretations of Scripture, politics, and the economy. We even had to deal with a member who was acting inappropriately and making some of the women uncomfortable.

We pray together, bring our worries to one another, and share our doubts and faltering. In the six months we've been together online, we've walked with each other through divorce, childbirth, a transcontinental move, career changes, financial problems, deaths of loved ones, family members going off to war, unemployment, sickness, injury, depression, parenting issues, and—perhaps one of our greatest challenges in keeping the community honest and safe *and* loving—the presidential election. Short of deciding which color to paint the narthex—pink or black seemed to be the most popular options—we function much like any church, warts and all. (And we have a lot of warts.)

Earlier this year, I read with interest Shane Hipps's Fermi Short titled, "Our Nomadic Existence: How Electronic Culture Shapes Community." In it, Shane expresses his concern not only for the method of electronic communication but also for the medium itself. He says, "If virtual community functions like cotton candy, then authentic community is more like broccoli. It may not always taste good, but it provides crucial nourishment for the formation of our identity. Authentic community will undoubtedly be marked by conflict, risk, and rejection. At the same time, it offers the deepest levels of acceptance, intimacy, and support."

Shane says he's not morally opposed to cotton candy, as it can serve a legitimate—if limited—place in a person's diet. "In the same way I am not morally opposed to virtual community; it also serves an important and limited function in our electronic culture," he says. "The problem is that virtual community is slowly becoming the preferred means of relating."

Now, I don't intend for this essay to be construed as a polemic in support or defense of virtual community and/or online spirituality. But I feel compelled to tell the story of an absolutely authentic, transformative phenomenon that has truly enlivened my faith. Caution is a natural reaction to systemic change in our culture, and surely the dawning of Web 2.0 is a real, live paradigm shift. If we all stopped talking to one another in person and only communicated through blips on a computer screen, humanity would suffer for it.

But I think it's equally dangerous to dismiss innovations in communication as frivolous or somehow fraudulent simply because they're different. Is there a risk involved in becoming more "digital" and less "analog"? Absolutely. But so too there is an opportunity for God to make something beautiful out of something if not ugly at least soulless. The God I know is the God of infinite possibility and unimaginable creativity. God can use whatever God wants to use to connect us not only to him but also to one another. When we open our hearts and minds to each other — whether face-to-face, in writing, in music, or in art — a sacred exchange takes place. In my experience, the community of believers can be just as authentic and grace filled, just as maddening and difficult, whether it is experienced in cyberspace or a cathedral.

As mentioned above, our virtual church is not immune to conflict, risk, and rejection. We've wrestled through all of that, and I'm sure we will continue to do so as long as we remain a community — virtual or not. Rather than replacing face-to-face interactions, the thread has for us been a blessing of addition, not subtraction. Would that we could all walk down the block and plop down in each other's living rooms. Unfortunately, we live all over the world, and so it's just not possible most of the time. Some of us do live near enough to spend physical time together — and we do. The Daves are only a few blocks apart, and more often than not, we know what they're having for dinner at whose house, and what wine they've decided to pair with it. Two of the women on the thread live in the same town where we all went to college, about a half hour from me in the suburbs of Chicago. The more we "talk" online, the more we've wanted to also talk in person. And we do. When we do, we've found that the face time is enriched by our shared cyberexistence.

Back in August, when my new book was released, my publisher

threw a party for me in Chicago. The thread knew about it — as there's not a whole lot about one another's quotidian and extraordinary lives that we don't talk about — and decided it was time for us to get together and share an actual meal, at an actual table, with actual wine. The Daves flew in from California, Susan drove up from St. Louis, Kathy flew in from New York City, Shani and Jen and their husbands made the short commute in from Wheaton, and James schlepped all the way to Chicago from Dubai. Yes, Dubai.

Some of us hadn't seen each other in almost twenty years. A few of us hadn't even met in person. I think we were all a bit nervous about whether the physical thread would be more awkward than the virtual thread. Happily, nothing could have been further from the truth. We clicked immediately, without a moment's hesitation. It was just like our daily conversations online, except the only things standing between us were wine goblets and a table, not a computer screen and thousands of miles.

At our dinner in Chicago that night, we were able to remember Mark together. An 8-by-10 framed portrait of the one I like to call "Sweet Face" sat on a special chair — the "grace chair" — festooned with brightly colored flowers and fig branches at the head of the table. We prayed together over the food, toasted each other, told stories, and laughed until we cried (and a few times cried until we laughed). We thanked one another for being grace for each other. We thanked God for our friendship and, yes, for Facebook.

The Daves asked me to get up and say a few words. I didn't know how to express all that I was feeling, but as I looked down the table of friends to glimpse Mark's picture in the grace chair, I knew what I wanted to say. What had begun with something ugly — grieving the unfathomable loss of our extraordinary friend — had turned into something magnificent. God, in his grace, does indeed make beauty out of ugly things. That night together, sharing a meal and the same physical space, was one of the most moving, blessed experiences of my life. We didn't want it to end, as evidenced by the fact that many of us stayed up until dawn talking, laughing, reminiscing, and making plans to see each other again in a different city on the East or West Coast as soon as we could swing it.

Rather than replace "actual" face-to-face community, the thread, in its virtual incarnation, makes us yearn to be in one another's company. I think that has fueled the passion with which we keep our cyberchurch going. When one or another of us is gone from Facebook for a few days, we miss each other. We ask where they've been. We go find each other. When I'm out traveling without a computer for a few days, I get a longing ache for my brothers and sisters online. I miss them. I want the contact—that authentic community. My spirit craves it.

For most of my life, I have been a member of a church. It was a given. But about a dozen years ago, the Episcopal congregation I called home had an acrimonious split over issues of homosexuality and scriptural authority, and I took a hiatus from church. Fellow churchgoers who judged one another mercilessly, making piety a competition and community too often a place where I felt the least safe, had spiritually injured me many times over the years. What started as a hiatus lasted until last month. I didn't intend for that to happen, but it did. Personal spiritual trauma combined with my given vocation—as a religion reporter I went to church for a living—made it difficult for me to turn off my inner critic whenever I visited a new church, searching for a home but never finding it.

Perhaps the most extraordinary product of virtual church is that it has led my husband and me back to a physical church. Jen, one of the women on the thread who lives a few suburbs away from me, is in love with her church. She speaks about it with such fondness and gratefulness, recounting interactions with fellow congregants and sharing the beauty of the priest's gentle, grace-filled ministry, that over time I became curious. Interestingly (God does have a tremendous sense of humor) hers is an Episcopal congregation that had endured a painful split a few years back over homosexuality and scriptural authority. After months of hearing about her spiritual home, I wanted to see what Jen was talking about for myself, setting aside my fears of getting hurt for the possibility I might once again embrace a local church home.

In October, my husband and I celebrated our eleventh wedding anniversary with Jen and her husband, David. We spent the night at their house and the next morning joined them and their four children for church. It just so happened the service we attended was a healing service, where any and all were invited to approach the altar for prayer. Surprising no one more than myself, I got up from the pew in the back of the sanctuary and walked up the aisle. When the priest approached me, asking what she could pray for, all I could articulate was, "So much. I'm just really broken." She placed her hands on my head and prayed for God to heal me in whatever ways I needed to be made whole. I got up from my knees, feeling somehow lighter and full of joy. Walking back to my seat, I caught Jen's eye. She was crying. That I couldn't have seen online, but I know deep in my soul that without Facebook, I would never have seen those tears in person. What amazing grace!

As I understand it, grace is a gift. It's something we can't earn or lose. We can't do anything to make us more or less worthy of

God's greatest gift to us. Grace is startling, wild, surprising, and life changing. A few years back, I had a conversation with the author Anne Lamott, who in books such as *Traveling Mercies* and *Grace (Eventually)* has spoken eloquently about the experience of God's audacious, unearnable gift. I asked her if she thought we could be grace for one another. "I think we can hold space for one another," Annie told me. Without my knowing it, Jen and David, and no doubt the rest of the thread, had been holding space for me until I was ready to move into it.

When I was a freshman at Wheaton, in an introduction to theology class I read a book by John V. Taylor called *The Go-Between God*. In it, Taylor argues that the Spirit of God can be experienced as much *between* people as in them. Perhaps the Spirit of God abides as well in the electrons that float through space when we email each other or post to the Facebook thread. Computers and the Internet may be the media, but the connectivity is altogether spiritual. Looked at it from that perspective, logging on takes on a new, profound meaning.

After all, there is no distance in the spirit. Even cyberspace can be a sacred space.

ABOUT CATHLEEN FALSANI

Cathleen Falsani, author of *Sin Boldly*, *The Dude Abides*, and *The God Factor*, is the award-winning religion columnist for the *Chicago Sun-Times*. She attended Wheaton College and holds master's degrees in journalism and theology. She lives in Laguna Beach, California, with her husband and fellow journalist, Maurice Possley.

Share Your Thoughts

With the Author: Your comments will be forwarded to the author when you send them to *zauthor@zondervan.com*.

With Zondervan: Submit your review of this book by writing to *zreview@zondervan.com*.

Free Online Resources at
www.zondervan.com

Zondervan AuthorTracker: Be notified whenever your favorite authors publish new books, go on tour, or post an update about what's happening in their lives.

Daily Bible Verses and Devotions: Enrich your life with daily Bible verses or devotions that help you start every morning focused on God.

Free Email Publications: Sign up for newsletters on fiction, Christian living, church ministry, parenting, and more.

Zondervan Bible Search: Find and compare Bible passages in a variety of translations at www.zondervanbiblesearch.com.

Other Benefits: Register yourself to receive online benefits like coupons and special offers, or to participate in research.